Australia and Indo-Pacific Defence: Anchoring a Way Ahead

Robbin F. Laird

Contents

This book is dedicated to my Australian mates John Blackburn and
Anne Borzycki with affection, admiration and respect.

Chapter One

Foreword

In *Australia and Indo-Pacific Defence: Anchoring a Way Ahead,* author and editor of over thirty books, Robbin Laird, brings to bear his expertise on defence and security affairs to make sense of contemporary Australian international security and defence policy. This is his third book focused on Australian defence. It reveals the sharp mind of a person very well connected in Australian defence policy, academic and military practitioner circles.

Laird has expertly sought to engage with and understand perspectives of Australian defence and security experts, many of whom are associated with the Williams Foundation, a not-for-profit Australian organisation established to advocate for the appropriate development and use of airpower, along with the other services, in defence of Australia and its interests.

This book echoes the work of the Williams Foundation which has encompassed reforms underway affecting the application not just of airpower, but also capabilities that apply to the maritime, land, space and cyber domains. It addresses the challenges of force modernisation and transformation in the context of fluctuating great power relativities (notably with the rise of an assertive and more confrontational China) in a dynamic Indo-Pacific region, at a time of significant policy initiatives affecting Australia and its place in the world. These initiatives notably include Australia's 2023 Defence Strategic Review (DSR) and the implementation of the Australia, United Kingdom United States (AUKUS) advanced technical sharing agreement, helping Australia to acquire nuclear propulsion submarines and other advanced military capabilities.

Laird taps into the insights of a wide range of defence and security experts including Marcus Hellyer, Andrew Shoebridge, Peter Jennings (formerly with the Australian Strategic Policy Institute, or ASPI); Andrew Dowse (RAND Australia); Andrew Carr, Stephan Fruehling, Paul Dibb, Richard Brabin-Smith, the late Brendan Sargeant, Alan Dupont, Ross Babbage and this writer (currently from or previously with the Strategic and Defence Studies Centre, or SDSC, at the Australian National University). Others scholars consulted include Harald Malmgren and Nicholas Linsman.

The perspectives of a significant number of current and former service personnel are woven into the narrative as well. These include Robert Chipman, John Blackburn, Darren Goldie, John Harvey and Michael Kitcher from the Royal Australian Air Force (RAAF); Tim Barrett and Darron Kavanagh from the Royal Australian Navy (RAN); Simon Stuart, Anthony Rawlins and David Beaumont from the Australian Army; and Mike Pezzullo from the Australian Public Service.

Renowned politics and international affairs commentator, Greg Sheridan, features also, as does the U.S. Navy 's Charles A. Richard. Australian defence industry leaders feature in the mix also; notably John Conway (Felix Defence), Matthew Wilson (Penten), Jason Scholz (Trusted Autonomous Systems defence Cooperation Centre) as well as Allan Paull (Defence Science and Technology Group) and Jake Campbell (Northrop Grumman Australia).

Laird also puts these perspectives in the context of the views of current and former political leaders like the late Senator (and retired Major General) Jim Molan, former Defence Minister and Australian Ambassador to the USA, Kim Beazley, Prime Minister Anthony Albanese, as well as Defence Minister and Deputy Prime Minster Richard Marles.

The book explores conceptual frameworks for thinking about Australia's defence considered at and around Williams Foundation seminars in 2022 and 2023. These include the strategic challenges faced due to the rise of China and the state of flux in the United States' economic strength, its political resolve and questions over its military preparedness associated with accelerated technological developments.

The book also considers issues arising from Australia's 'paradox': its attempts to reconcile its history and its geography and the striving for a variety of regional partners, including in the Association of Southeast Asian Nations (ASEAN), the Pacific island forum (PIF), AUKUS, the Quad (alongside India, Japan and the USA); its sense of being an island continent (or an 'archipelago'); the changing nature of the Chinese challenge, or 'co-opetition' posed by authoritarian powers; the paradox of living dependent on seaborne trade and thus vulnerable to the influence of a foreign power that does not need to invade Australia to defeat it; and the challenge of effective deterrence that avoids escalation.

Laird also considers recent and forecast precision and longer range weapons systems acquisitions, the rotation of U.S. forces in and through Australia, the challenges of supply chain resilience and weapons stockpiles, artificial intelligence, robotics and unattended vehicles, the politics and policy ingredients and technical difficulties that come with AUKUS.

Laird further observes 'The ADF is a modest force well trained in coalition operations', but requires some work to best be able to operate from the Australian 'sanctuary'. He makes some important observations: The Australian Army, given its operation of the lands, is the key force in terms of working in the neighbourhood' (notably on regional defence diplomacy); the [RAN] faces a major challenge in terms of sorting out the mix and match of platforms'; and the 'RAAF remains the tip of the spear'.

This is an important book by a very well connected, informed and astute observer of Australia's circumstances as they pertain to defence challenges, U.S. alliance dynamics, and technological as well as policy and political hurdles.

His conclusion points to the utility of this book in shedding light on finding solutions to key defence challenges centred around the notion of 'Archipelagic Deterrence':

"[Australia] needs a defence policy that fits this period of global upheaval. In my view, it is by becoming more resilient and doing so by being interactive with and driving change amongst its allies to shape credible paths to more resilience in the face of the authoritarian powers that it provides a leadership role...

"Australia's archipelagic Deterrence strategy represents a more stable and resilient alignment of interests and capabilities between Canberra and Washington than forward leaning alternatives. Australian leaders may talk loudly about pan-regional and global contributions however the enduring logic of the nation's force structure and posture has always been territorial security. The DSR reinforces that tradition..."

Defence practitioners, strategist and policy makers will find this book a rich resource.

John Blaxland

Professor of International Security and Intelligence Studies, Strategic and Defence Studies Centre, Coral Bell School of Asia Pacific Affairs, College of Asia and the Pacific, Australian National University

25 June 2023

Chapter Two

Introduction

In my 2020 book on Australian defence, I focused on the drive to enhance the ability of the Australian Defence Force (ADF) to operate as an integrated force. It is and was a work in progress but has been enhanced by the current government's clear recognition of the threat which China poses in the Indo-Pacific region.

I concluded the book with my assessment of the Australian effort to shape a way ahead.

"I have been coming to Australia since 2014 and have written the reports for the Williams Foundation seminars held twice a year in that time. We began with the issue of airpower modernization and the impact of the F-35 upon airpower modernization, and, over time, that has broadened to Australian Defence Force modernization.

"And that focus has been upon leveraging the world's most modern air force to drive transformation of the ADF to become a fifth-generation force. Building a fifth-generation force has revolved around building an integrated force that can operate in a very flexible distributed manner.

"This effort with the Williams Foundation has encompassed the broader transformation process of the Army, the Navy, as well as the Maritime Border Command. It has not been a narrowly focused discussion but one that has discussed, debated, and highlighted the significant force modernization issues arising from the shift from the engagement in Middle Eastern land wars to returning to the Pacific and having to consider what the rise of the twenty-first-century authoritarian powers and their military modernization efforts mean for Australia and its allies.

"As this effort has progressed, the strategic environment itself has been changing, even dramatically. The year 2014 was certainly key in terms of the impact of not only the seizure of Crimea by the Russians from Ukraine, but also the destruction by the Russians of Malaysia Airlines Flight 17 while flying over eastern Ukraine. With 2014 opening up a new strategic era, other changes were in train, ranging from the Chinese build-out into the Pacific, to the European crisis associated with Brexit and the migration crises generated from the Middle East, notably the ISIS and Syrian wars, to the coming to power of President Trump and the opening of a new strategic debate in the United States about the way ahead for American power, and to the reconsideration by Australia of what exactly is the nature of their strategic neighborhood and how best to proceed.

"And now we have the Coronavirus crisis, which certainly has accelerated discussions and hopefully decisions on how to determine the way ahead on various security issues, including those regarding supply chains.

"As we worked the broader military transformation assessments, the aperture was widening with regard to how best to defend Australia, work with its closest allies, and protect Australian sovereignty. This started first with considerations with regard to how to sustain the ADF in times of crisis. What defence industrial capabilities or defence stockpiles does Australia need to have in country to cope with and prevail in a crisis situation involving the authoritarian powers who have the capability to disrupt supply lines into Australia?

"The logistics and sustainment discussions have broadened into discussions about the return of geography. With the Chinese pushing out from the mainland and shaping a phased island strategy, their ability to project power out into the Pacific raises again the question of the role of Australian territory, notably Western Australia and the Northern territories, in the defence of Australia. An enhanced role for these territories in extended deterrence is a distinct possibility for the ADF going forward.

"Some in Australia would see this as a Fortress Australia policy, but it is really something quite different. It is about whether the ADF can operate from Western Australia and the Northern territories much more flexibly and do so as if the territory operated a chessboard across which forces could be moved in a crisis.

"There is the question of the ability of the Australian forces to do so. RAAF will certainly look at agile basing and enhanced capabilities to operate from a variety of airstrips and mobile bases. The Navy already operates their submarine force from Western Australia, and as the new build submarines are added to the force, flexibility might be considered in regards to operating the force, somewhat similar to how Australia operated in World War II."

That was a pretty accurate picture of where the Australian defence debate was going. We have entered a new strategic era in which the dynamics within the liberal democracies are being shaped in interaction with the conflict with the twenty-first-century authoritarian powers. The individual nations within the "free world" are clearly in flux and with regard to their alliances and working relationships.

The United States is no longer the superpower of the 1950s or that of the nation leading in the wake of the collapse of the Soviet Union or the reunification of Germany. Its power has declined relative to a world in which several power centres have emerged. The prospect of a global order enforcing a "rules-based order" is more distant now.

This new context for Australia means that it has been thrust into a world in change, and one in which it will have to take more responsibility for its own defence. But this is occurring as the challenges associated with security and defence are widening and broadening, with cyber war, hybrid warfare, and grey zones being coined as phrases to grasp the new situation.

In this companion book to *Joint By Design*, I am going to look at developments since 2020, mirrored in the Williams Foundation seminars, which began again after the pandemic, but I will first start with my first three chapters which address the question of the transition prior to the Australian Defence Strategic Review being released on 24 April 2023. The interviews for these first three chapters were conducted in 2022 with the other chapters informed by interviews as late as April 2023 along with follow-up phone interviews until the publication of this book.

Chapter Three

The ADF and Australian Direct Defence

The direct defence of Australia is a major shift in the focus and priorities for the ADF. The ADF has built a force which can deploy an independent task force for the nation by air or sea. This effort over the past decade provides a basis for working the way ahead.

Eighty percent of the force that the nation will have in twenty years' time, it has now. What changes will have to be made to redeploy that force? What changes can be made in the next three to five years to increase the lethality and survivability force? What changes will be made to the force to reach the areas of broader strategic interest of Australia?

What Will Have to Change?

In providing some answers to this question, I talked with Dr. Marcus Hellyer, formerly of the Australian Strategic Policy Institute and now with Strategic Analysis, Australia. Hellyer started with a very fundamental question: "What is the Australian Defence Force (ADF) purpose-built for?" And here he posed what is becoming a clear choice: Is the ADF for the away game or for primary defence of the Australian continent?"

This is how he put it: "Is the purpose for the ADF essentially to defend the Australian continent, or is it about going wherever in the world we need to go with our allies and addressing threats and the issues of the day, wherever that may be around the world?"

He argued that the existing force structure clearly is designed for the latter. "I would argue that the ADF is essentially designed to plug into a coalition, obviously led by the U.S., and go wherever in the world we think we need to address a threat or the issue of the day. And that's the only way I can really make any sense of our existing force structure."

But with the United States facing its own domestic and foreign policy challenges, the United States is facing *capacity constraints*. "It can't be everywhere at the same time. We recognize that the U.S. is essentially telling its allies that and telling them to step up. Ultimately, I think that's what AUKUS is about. We actually need to do some hard thinking and be a little less complacent about our defence. And that means prioritizing the things that ADF absolutely must do."

If Australia is to focus on its own defence and defence in depth, that raises the question of the nature of the defence perimeter for Australia which the ADF and the nation need to address. And that would mean as well that Australia would be less focused on the away game in the Pacific and by shaping defence in depth, they could offer a defence sanctuary for allies like Japan or the United States, but at the expense of what at least some U.S. decision-makers wish to see which would be the Quad forces are operating closer to Chinese territory.

Hellyer argued that with the forces already in being and the forces that can be built out, a reasonable objective for Australian defence is to operate more effectively out to Australia's first island chain or in an arc from the Solomon Islands across the north coast of New Guinea and the Indonesian archipelago. He underscored: "I think we need to be able to indicate to a potential adversary that this area would be a very dangerous space for them to be operating in. And that's where I would be conceptually prioritizing effort, as opposed to say the South China Sea."

Rather than building and supporting a balanced force structure, given financial and manpower constraints, a priority might be placed on the ADF forces which have the greatest combat or crisis management effect for the direct defense of Australia within the defence arc highlighted by Hellyer. It is a question of investing in the force that makes the biggest difference in the shortest period of time.

We concluded by discussing the build out of balanced force or a threat-based force. Hellyer argued: "I think you'll find that countries that are facing a very clear threat don't do capability-based planning, they do threat-based planning to counter that threat. And I think the time has come to get back to your initial point about what's the key thinking we need to change here? Do we actually need to move to more of a threat-based planning, because there is a clear threat?

"What are the capabilities you need that can defeat that threat, or certainly complicate how that threat is going to approach us? And we need to build forces that are relevant to the threat we face and our efforts to build out our direct defence of Australia."

Redeploying the Force

The question of redeployment is a question of geography and what kind of force disposition gives you the most force efficacity: how can the force be best deployed to be most relevant to the crisis facing Australia? How to distribute the force for survivability and yet have the C2 system to deliver the level of integrated effect required?

A good way to conceptualise the strategic geography for the ADF was suggested by Dr. Andrew Carr of Australian National University in an interview conducted for this book. Given the enhanced focus on the direct defence of Australia being generated with the evolving strategic environment, Dr. Carr provided an assessment of this shift and how it fit into the longer-term perspective of threats, challenges, and Australian defence policy seen in the longer term.

According to Carr, "Australians actually have quite a long history of thinking about how to defend our country, obviously in very different circumstances, but certainly weighing how to balance what we need to do here on the continent versus what we need to do with partners.

"We've always had a tension between the two. And I think it's underappreciated how much Australians actually have been concerned about direct defence. For example, in 1903, when our first defence act was passed, it actually forbade the professional force from going overseas because the defence forces were for coastal and port defences. That's why we had these giant volunteer forces engaged in the First World War.

"I think the public image of Australia always racing overseas to fight with allies and other people's wars is a mistaken view. I think there is a longer history of Australians thinking seriously about our direct defence. And often that thinking isn't done in public due to alliance sensitivities, but we are now seeing more willingness to do so."

What Carr was underscoring was the need to balance support for allies, notably a primary ally. This primary ally was initially, the United Kingdom and then the United States, with the needs for Australian direct defence. Clearly, allies are important for a credible direct defence of Australia, but what one might call a necessary but not sufficient condition for ensuring credible direct defence of the continent. Carr characterised this question of balance as "transactional if not even Machiavellian in the way that they've tried to manage those alliance relationships and balancing between what we thought was essential for our own security and what we thought we needed to do or wanted to do with our partners."

He then drew an example from the Second World War: "Robert Menzies, at the start of the Second World War, stated that as a consequence of Britain being at war, we're at war. But then spent the first three months of the conflict telling the British we're not sending forces, we're not going overseas because we are worried about the Japanese, and we are worried about your commitment to our region, and we are clearly worried about our own homeland security. And once he gets a better sense of what the Japanese might do, then he's willing to commit to significant overseas cooperation."

The Indonesian conflict from 1963 to 1966 was also a clear element of understanding that the nature of the challenges involved the nature of direct defence of Australia. Carr underscored that the nature of the threats in the region rapidly dominated the Australian defence focus and re-oriented the calculus for force structure development. "Suddenly the Australian government changes completely what it's spending its money on, what kind of forces it was buying, it's willingness to spend money, with our defence becoming nearly 17% of the national budget. And we bought equipment such as the Oberon submarines and ultimately the F-111s and made a number of procurement decisions that really are at the heart of what the ADF is today because of that concern for the continent. In other words, the Indonesian conflict had much more of an impact on Australian force structure and military thinking than Vietnam did, even though that was much more publicly controversial and historically seen as the key moments in the Cold War."

We then discussed a key concept in Dr. Carr's work, namely, how to think about Australia's strategic geography in relationship to its defence focus. This is how he had put it: "There is an underlying paradox of is Australia an island or a continent? Determining your focus has important implications for the kinds of defence forces you want to build and the way you think about your relationship with others and the role of the state. We go back to Athens and Sparta, the one a land power, and the other a sea power, and they fought in different ways, and they created very different kinds of empires. In the 1980s, when Australia was thinking seriously about home defence and how you would build a force structure for that, the implicit idea was that Australia was an island.

"We focused on the SE gap to our north, on long-range under-standing of traffic that might come down through the first island chain, developing JORN, the Jindalee Operational Radar Network, and other systems like that for understanding that environment. Our maritime focus drove a lot of our defence policies. There was actually very little conception about how we would us Australia's own geog-raphy for your advantage in a way that the Chinese or the Russians as classic continental powers have done so. And that was appropriate for the time and circumstances.

"There are examples of Australians in a crisis thinking about how to leverage our continental advantages. The classic examples is the Second World War, where in desperation we suddenly considered whether Australia needed to develop an insurgent or gorilla strategy with the public volunteering to fight the Japanese if they landed in Australia.

"Could we trade space for time? But the Australian continent isn't very useful for such an approach because all of our key population and industrial centers are along the coast often with a mountain range very close to the coast with the result that we are clustered near the sea in de facto 'island chains.'"

Carr then argued that there was a third approach to conceptualising Australia's strategic geography which suggests a way to conceptualise the way ahead for Australian direct defence. "If you look at where people have lived since British invasion in 1788 on this continent, it's closer to being an archipelagic nation. You have the island of Sydney, the island of Melbourne, the island of Tasmania, the island of Brisbane and Darwin, with vast gaps in between.

"Our early patterns of settlement were all about supporting these distinct islands. The Australians didn't run railways across the continent and have an expanding frontier as the Americans had. Everything ran to the sea because economically it made more sense to send goods to the nearest port, and then send it by ship from city to city, island to island effectively, or off to America or to Europe for trade.

"In other words, we have an archipelagic country that has very distinct cultures that are also connected and for a defence perspective, that leads to a different way of operating or thinking about your ability to move across and between settlements. Rather than being tied to the direct defence of every specific inch of territory. How do we extract benefit from such an approach? How can we move force between sea and lands seamlessly and recognize that it's not simply the defence of your territory but having the ability to move out into the region in cooperation with partners and allies, where Indonesia is the largest traditional archipelago in the world? There are many significant archipelagic nations in the South Pacific, and we are going to need an ADF that is able to operate seamlessly across those environments as well."

This means working mobile basing, force mobility, agile combat employment, and leveraging land, sea, and air bases to concentrate force against key threats in the region—and with the autonomous revolution at hand, finding ways to get enhanced mass of payloads in support of the missions from a diversity of uncrewed as well as crewed platforms.

Conceptualising of Australia in archipelago terms raises the question of rethinking the ADF as an archipelago defence-capable ADF and as such can help both in restructuring the ADF in the near to midterm and also providing a sense of priorities for defence modernisation and what mobilisation of the nation might need to look like going forward.

The RAAF Rethinks Its Positioning

Two 2022 presentations provide a good sense of the RAAF leadership perspective on the shift which the RAAF needs to make to facilitate the direct defence of Australia. Both were made at The Williams Foundation Seminar on the way ahead for defence in the new strategic context, and the major presentation by the head of the RAAF, Air Marshal Robert Chipman, was supplemented by an interview done for this book.

In his remarks at the September 28, 2022, Williams Foundation seminar, Chipman explained the shift as follows: "As we consider strategies to deter conflict in the Indo-Pacific region, we should consider how we might contain conflict geographically and/or within specific domains. And what actions might lead to runaway escalation."

With the return to a priority on the direct defence of Australia, albeit in a broader alliance context, "geography should shape our approach to national security. The ability to deliver effects at a distance from our territory, and in the approaches Australian sovereign territory will be a critical feature of our future security strategy. Air power will make a vital contribution to our joint force structure and posture in this context."

But he warned that the traditional view of the strategic geography has been modified by technological and warfighting advances. "Our traditional view of a contest in the physical domains is obsolete. Operations in and through the space and cyber domains have extended Australia's strategic geography. They don't displace the maritime, land and air domains, but rather demand a lift in our capacity to contest them all, and importantly, integrate our warfighting effects between them in order to conduct joint all-domain operations."

With regard to lethality, the air force can deploy with longer range weapons in the near term. "The Long-Range Anti-Ship Missile (LRASM), a modern fifth-generation weapon, will soon enhance the lethality of our Super Hornet and P-8A's maritime strike capabilities. It is an investment that will help Australia avoid coercion, protect our sea lines of communication, and assure maritime security in our region. It will be complemented by the Joint Air-to-Surface Standoff Missile–Extended Range (JASSM-ER), another variant of the AGM-158 family of missiles that will enable our Super Hornets, and in future, our F-35As to engage targets at ranges exceeding 900 km. These weapons will be supported by a joint ISR and targeting enterprise, integrated with our allies and partners, to enable precision long range fires. As we introduce this capability into service, we will continually revisit the robustness of this enterprise, the sufficiency of our war stock and the resilience of our logistics arrangements to sustain the capability."

At the same time, the survivability of the force needs to be enhanced as well through an emphasis on mobility and resilience. Air Marshal Chipman underscored that in order to project power from Australia, "we must address the resilience of our air bases, supporting infrastructure, C2, and of course our fuel and explosive ordnance to sustain air and space operations. To force generate the resilience we need to fight with degraded systems in contested environments."

The resilience piece needs to be driven by innovations that derive from an effort to "imagine how we will sustain and project air and space power against an adversary capable of exploiting our vulnerabilities in all domains. "However, if the present monopolises our thinking, we simply stay the execution. There is a future of hypersonic missiles, directed energy weapons, artificial intelligence and swarming unmanned systems that is also racing towards us. We must deal with both realities and manage strategic risk over time. We must ensure our strategy, capability and resources are harmonised and deliver an air and space force with the right balance of protection, agility, lethality, and survivability."

Air Marshal Chipman noted in an interview held the day after his presentation to the conference: "We need to focus on ways to enhance dispersion, agility, movement, and manoeuvre as a force. We need to understand how we will manoeuvre as an air force and that encompasses the ground and air infrastructure that's required to do that. And we need to manoeuvre as a joint force. We need to have a joint scheme of manoeuvre that involves both ground and air elements. And in building out the ADF as a joint force, the challenge is to enhance the readiness and capabilities of the current joint force to deliver enhanced capabilities for the direct defence of Australia but at the same time position the ADF for force modernization and capability enhancements."

Air Marshal Chipman underscored: "We will fight with what we've got today. And for the next 20 years, possibly up to 80% of our future order of battle will have already been fielded today. But if you look at the quality of our platforms and the quality of the training and the quality of our people, then we're as well placed for a nation of our size as we could be with our air power, with what we've got today."

But the challenge can be put this way. He noted: "It's how we use air power to achieve that agility, how we use it to make sure that we are survivable and that we can get mass to the right point when we need it to influence the battle space. It's that approach that we are changing with our focus on force agility. We are focused on agile combat employment and thinking about dispersal, moving quickly, moving lightly, even with F-35, taking small numbers of maintainers and less support equipment than we would typically require at a major base. Our approach will take us to a kill web environment, but we will be looking for ways to accelerate our mission threads in such an environment and we'll be looking for ways to make sure any new capabilities are integrated and operational as quickly as possible.

"And the two areas that are of greatest focus to me are integrated air missile defence and space. With the integrated air and missile defence piece, there's a lot of opportunity to work with Army. With regard to the space domain, we are focused on the evolving interfaces between air and space. With effective integration, we can have joint fire systems so that I can achieve effects throughout the joint force from common systems. I believe that the integrated air missile defence project is a genuine step along our pathway to fielding a kill web."

The way Chipman put it was clearly reworking the current force to provide a proper template for any force modernisation or enhancements to follow. And doing so meant that Australia was looking to do so in ways that could intersect like a Venn Diagram with its allies to get the most effective feasible integrability possible without compromising the survival of the combat force in critical combat conditions.

Take the case of Agile Combat Employment (ACE) or put another way, working ways to operate the RAAF throughout Australian territory in ways that would allow for its survival but to intersect beyond the continent in ways that mesh with the USAF's approach to ACE as well. As AVM Darren Goldie, Air Commander Australia, put it during his presentation at the Williams Foundation Seminar: "I've tasked the Air Warfare Centre with developing agile concepts with attendant risk consideration. We need to complicate an adversary's targeting process and create operational and political dilemmas for those that seek to disrupt our operations. There must be congruence with the USAF's agile combat employment or ACE . . . But this is specific Australian planning in recognition of our strategic geography."

The USAF and the RAAF approaches can be complimentary but have differences as well. Reworking force dispersal as well as the C2 to allow for Australian strategic depth have elements very different from a USAF trying work globally. Notably, the USAF is working a global concept of Joint All-Domain Command and Control. "Joint All-Domain Command and Control (JADC2) is the Department of Defence's (DOD's) concept to connect sensors from all of the military services—Air Force, Army, Marine Corps, Navy, and Space Force—into a single network."

But network sharing across a global system would be very complicated, and frankly, distributed force operations really are about how the modular task force at the tactical edge integrates effectively for combat or crisis effects, more than they are about how such an ACE force needs to reach back to a CAOC in Hawaii.

With regard to the USAF approach to ACE, the PACAF Commander, General Wilsbach, who has been a key participant in Williams Foundation seminars for many years, identified how he sees the way ahead. This is what he argued at the seminar: "One way the U.S. is responding to the challenges of PRC technological advancement is through continued refinement of the ACE concept. ACE ensures we are ready for potential contingencies by enabling our forces to effectively operate from numerous locations with varying levels of capacity and support. ACE's heartbeat is a network of well-established and austere air bases, prepositioned equipment, and airlift to rapidly deploy, disperse and maneuver combat capability throughout the region. As a coalition force, we must continue to expand our access, airspace, basing and resources west of the international dateline to better posture our sales to conduct distributed operations both during training and real-world missions."

What Wilsbach means was given more detail in an interview which I conducted at the PACAF headquarters in Honolulu in August 2021. Brigadier General Michael Winkler, then director of Strategic Plans, Requirements and Programs at the Pacific Air Force, provided this explanation of ACE: "PACAF has taken a realistic approach that is fiscally informed because it would be very difficult for us to try to build multiple bases with 10,000-foot runways, and dorms, and ammunition storage all over the Pacific. What we've done instead is to concentrate on a hub and spoke mentality, where you build a base cluster. That cluster has got a hub that provides quite a bit of logistic support to these different spoke airfields. The spokes are more expeditionary than most folks in the Air Force are used to. The expeditionary airfield is a spoke or a place that we operate from. It's not 10,000 feet of runway; it's maybe 7,000 feet. We're probably not going to have big munitions storage areas, there's probably going to be weapons carts that have missiles on them inside of sandbag bunkers. And we're going to look a lot more like a Marine Expeditionary base than your traditional big Air Force base. It'll be fairly expeditionary."

It is not obvious that this is how the RAAF will address force distribution within the Australian continent. But here it is very clear that how the Australian Army and the RAAF find ways to work together to provide for base mobility is at the heart of the way ahead for both the passive and active defence of Australian air bases.

The Royal Australian Navy and Its Way Ahead

In an interview conducted for this book, Vice Admiral (Retired) Tim Barrett, one of the key architects for the development of the Royal Australian Navy, provided insights concerning the way ahead for the RAN in the priority on direct defence of Australia. The changes already put in motion by the 2016 strategic review clearly needed to be accelerated but the threat envelope since that time had expanded rapidly in the region which has significant impacts on how to build, operate, and sustain the fleet.

The key shift has been from the Middle East to the Indo-Pacific region. Barrett noted: "By the time of the 2016 defence white paper, we had already assessed that our time in the Middle East was coming to an end. We'd had almost a continuous presence in that region for several decades, and that needed to change to a focus on the Indo-Pacific region."

But it is not simply about taking the assets that were deployed to the Middle East region and redeploying them to Australia's region. It is about the need as well to focus on the whole of nation defence approach. This is how Barrett put it: "The whole of nation appeal is not just about the navy itself. It's about the broad concept of providing a secure and assured supply chain to Australia, some of which will be to build the sovereign military capability, but a lot of it will be to sustain and defend the national economy."

We discussed a number of key aspects of shaping a way ahead for Australian maritime capabilities seen in terms of the national approach to defence, in terms of integration with the joint force, and in terms of working with allies. In particular, we discussed two key aspects of shaping a national approach to defence.

The first is the question of the build out of the Royal Australian Navy on Australian soil. How will Australia build out naval bases going forward? Will they co-locate sustainment locations with bases? How will they work forward sustainment efforts in the region and how will that correlate with sustainment and repair facilities within Australia itself? How will the approach to building out of Australian naval bases intersect with allied operations?

These issues obviously are a key part of the coming of the nuclear submarine capability to be deployed from Australia itself, but equally apply to the question of having the kind of basing infrastructure which credibly intersects with the challenge of staffing and quality of life that is crucial to attract the civilian workforce which is necessary for the kind of support the RAN needs for operations.

And as Australia builds parts of its fleet, how will those capabilities intersect with sustainment and repair for the fleet, including with regard to allied combat ships as well?

The second is the question of building Australian merchant marine capabilities. Barrett noted that "there are just 14 ships that are flagged on the Australian Register, and that number is going to decline over the next couple of years. The significance of flagging them under our register is that you have legal means by which you can requisition those ships to be able to take steps to secure fuel, to secure medical supplies, to secure fertilizers, whatever it may well be that you need in a crisis. You cannot do that if they're not on our register.

"Importantly, it also builds a level of trained workforce that will operate those ships in times of emergency, because we have a diminishing pool of competent mariners in Australia, some of whom need to be retained for a growing navy force, but we also need to retain them to fill merchant marine positions. But they're also the same people who manage ports and harbors, who manage all the ancillary facilities that are needed to supply a regular maritime industry."

By contrast, China has built a powerful commercial maritime enterprise which it has leveraged for its naval combat fleet as well. According to Barrett: "China produces more merchant ships per year than South Korea and Japan combined. It's been an overt practice, and they have not just a maritime fleet that exceeds all others, but their ownership of the entire integrated maritime industry has them owning more containers than others, has them managing more container ports around the world than others, has them managing a far greater level of maritime industry financing. If they don't own the ship, they probably own the financing behind why others own it, so therefore can influence behavior. And the quality of their warships that are being built now reflects their efforts in the commercial shipbuilding area as well."

We then discussed the way ahead with regard to the Australian combat fleet. VADM (retired) Barrett, when he was chief of navy, focused on the importance of integrated combat systems across the fleet. Such an approach also allows for enhanced integrability with allied fleets and with the joint force.

Notably, in the first ship to be built under the new continuous shipbuilding approach, the Arafura-class offshore patrol vessel, the combat systems are designed to operate modular capabilities onboard the ship and to integrate across the fleet. As Australia builds out its maritime autonomous systems capabilities, ships like the new class OPV can become mother ships delivering capabilities for the joint or allied forces.

The approach for the RAN in Barrett's view is as follows: "The ability of managing the combat system across the fleet means that you can vary what the hull or what the ship class can do for you and where it's likely to operate, but still retain that ability to connect and operate under a single combat plan. If you make that combat system interchangeable with your key allies, the U.S. in this region in particular, then it allows you to offer government far more creative options depending on what the threat is in the region. You don't necessarily put your air warfare destroyers or high value frigates to an area where you might be served by an OPV, which has a good combat system and a capability to modularize the weapons that it might be carrying. It can do work in that area to be able to demonstrate presence, particularly to the island nations, but also work from a deterrence point of view against someone who might seek to displace Australian interest in those areas. In other words, we're building a fleet that has more adaptability and that allows us to be more flexible in our operational responses, both from a national sovereignty point of view or an allied operational point of view. You can't do that with a fleet that's designed around single platform, single class types, proprietary combat systems and weapon systems that don't contribute to an overall arsenal that belongs to a modular task force. It's a philosophy as much as anything else, and I'd call it the Aegis lifestyle. You need to be able to operate in a way that you are a contributor to the overall modular task group. You all have the same ability to plug, play and contribute to the fight."

The then new head of the Royal Australian Navy (RAN) provided at the September 2022 Williams Seminar several guidelines concerning his own thinking about the way ahead for the RAN in the era of priority on direct defence Australia but in alliance context. According to VADM Mark Hammond: "The ability to sustain economic well-being while fighting is absolutely key, and as an island nation we will rely on both stockpiles onshore and imports across the seas. The right balance of capabilities to ensure national resilience through this phase is crucial. This system connects us globally—for better and for worse—is the key factor that enables Australia's prosperity and provides us with the ability to build infrastructure like hospitals, schools and sporting facilities. But it is also liable to the impacts of distant events such as war between nations, natural disasters and pandemics.

"Against this backdrop this government will decide the role of the ADF, what we will defend and where; what force we must project and where . . . and for how long; and who we must integrate with due to common purpose and shared interests to allow us to generate military force in the national interest. This will allow us to generate military advice to inform their decisions.

"This begs a number of questions. So what is the vital terrain requiring defence? Is it the rules-based system? Is it physical infrastructure or people? Is it information? Is it all of the above? If it is seabed infrastructure, is it in deep water or shallow water? Is it above water terminations? Is it in international or sovereign domains, or is it privately owned? It underpins our economic well-being—how important is it? What about merchant shipping? Whose flag, what cargo, where, when, for how long? And what about the ports and their maritime approaches? Which ports—ours, overseas, how many, for how long, from what? All or just some?

"If we protect and assure these things, do we assure our economic well-being? Only then we can ask, what is it that we need to do or have, to allow us to hold at risk or to undermine in order to defeat an adversary? Do we focus on our approaches or theirs, or both? Is it a manned systems problem or a job for robots? Do we need to project and protect a land force or a swarm of things? Or both? If so, in what phase of the conflict and with what risk appetite? How will we do this? Will it tip the balance in our nation's favour?"

How you answer these questions will guide you in your force development choices. Do you build your ships in Australia? Or take advantage of the work in European or Asian yards? Will Australia do like the Danes and take advantage of the next generation of modularity in shipbuilding? Will Australia break away from traditional ship classes? What role will maritime autonomous systems play in the distributed maritime force? For what missions? With what payloads? How will the RAAF and the RAN shape their collaboration and integration? What will be the relationship built between sea bases and RAAF agile combat employment? Will arsenal ships or planes be built or both?

In a discussion in the follow-up to the September 2022 seminar with Marcus Hellyer, we focused on alternative ways to build out the fleet as suggested by the choices embodied in these questions. We discussed the potential role of autonomous systems as a force extender for the manned platforms operating in an extended battlespace. He argued: "If you focus on unmanned or autonomous systems doing roles such as ISR and flooding the battle space with sensors, it allows the expensive exquisite platforms that we have in very small numbers, to be more effective. And also raises the question over time of the correct balance between rapid build systems like Unmanned Surface Vessels

(USVs) and the actual size of the fleet necessary for more expensive capital ships, for example."

I have done a great deal of research which has focused on how capital ships can be reimagined as mother ships and to leverage unmanned or automatous systems in new ways to extend the reach of those capital ships and making them more survivable and lethal. Hellyer highlighted one way ahead along these lines: "When the new OPV enters service next year, I wouldn't start using it as a large patrol boat. I would simply hand it over immediately for experimentation in that mothership role that we've both spoken about. Just say, 'Here, we've got this great tool with a lot of potential to be that mothership for unmanned underwater vessels, unmanned surface vessel, unmanned aerial vessels,' and get it out there and give it to the smart men and women who are going to use it and let them invent new ways to use this capability."

As Hammond concluded his presentation: "Lethality is the ability to deliver a decisive force against an adversary where it generates the greatest leverage. In the Australian context, with limited assets it is about maximum return on investment and maximising value for money as we deliver our desired effect. We cannot do everything, and we cannot sustain an attritional conflict.

"We cannot afford to take note of what of what 'everyone else' is doing and simply follow the path of the past. Neither can we simply look to a new capability to solve all problems. We are a small country with a small defence force. We need to generate maximum military power for every dollar of our taxpayer's money that we possibly can.

He concluded on a key point about innovation and training: "Our lethality will not be delivered only through buying new platforms. To use a historical example: in 1945 Japan lost the ability to exploit the natural resources that she needed to continue the war against the

United States, predominantly because her merchant shipping transiting her sea lines of communication had been decimated by American submarines. U.S. submariners had achieved decisive results against Japan, whereas their German U-boat 'peers' ultimately failed in the same mission against Britain in both world wars.

"While technology advances certainly assisted the U.S., no specific technology proved decisive in its own right. What is seldom effectively highlighted, is the fact that U.S. submariners seized and maintained their advantage against Japan by applying new technologies and tactics at a rate that continually mitigated their own weaknesses, targeted the enemy's and capitalised on their own strengths. This was done as part of global campaign of allied nations, working together as an integrated and joint force to destroy the capacity and will of another nation to continue a conflict."

The Australian Army on New Path?

In many ways, the Australian Army faces the biggest changes in the ADF in a strategic shift in Australian defence. If the primary purpose of the ADF is to work within a whole of nation approach to direct defence of Australia, where does the Army deploy and prepare to operate?

In some ways, it becomes the key support force for the RAAF. If indeed the shift of the RAAF is to deploy from Northern or Western Australia, how will the Army assist? What will be its role in defending fixed air bases? Standing up and supplying mobile air bases? What is its role in missile defence in the most relevant or priority defence regions of Australia? With regard to the Navy, the launch of maritime remote systems within key maritime zones will grow. Who will handle the C2 and the national warning grid? Is the Army best placed to do so?

Indeed, what will the Army's role be in homeland direct defence? How could it build the most relevant reserve structure? Are there lessons to be learned from Finland, for example, in terms of how to mobilise society with the Army leading the way?

What is the role of the Army in the littoral regions in the territory North of the island continent? Does the Army become more like the U.S. Marines? Do they need Ospreys rather than slow-moving helicopters? What is the role for heavy armour in the Army's future? What is the role for artillery—notably longer-range artillery—in the littoral regions with sufficient provision of ammunition for them? Does the Army prepare to deploy in effect kill boxes into the littoral region to make operating in Australia's first island chain simply not worth the military effort? What is the role of the Australian Army in building partnerships in the region? How effectively could it deploy in the region as part of an integrated ADF?

The Chief of the Army, Lieutenant General Simon Stuart, is certainly well aware of the challenges facing the Army in its transition and discussed these in a 2022 interview with me. At the heart of any change is determining how best to work with the joint force in the direct defence of Australia, which includes significant demands to operate in the littoral regions adjacent to Australia and out into relevant areas of the Pacific.

We started by discussing the strategic environment. Lieutenant General Stuart underscored that Australia was a middle power, not a great power. This means that working with allies and partners in the region effectively was a core competence which the Army needs to develop, enhance, and maximise. He argued that their exercise regimes in the region as well as working with Pacific partners was a key part of this effort. He argued that, "We are a convening power. What is our strategy? Fundamentally it comes down to working with the alliance we have with the United States and other like-minded states, to promote shared interests. And in those contexts, we are focused on being a net contributor to alliance security as well as our own. And we are addressing how we work together to build the interior lines of defence in the region—to use land—in Indo-Pacific defence."

How do you further enhance and develop such an approach? According to Lieutenant General Stuart, "You take the architecture that already exists through the multilateral activities we do with Indonesia on activities like Garuda Shield, Balikatan with the Philippines, Cobra Gold in Thailand, Talisman Saber in Australia. You build those out as multilateral activities and connect them in a way that strengthens international partnerships while enabling a persistent multilateral presence. And that persistent presence and multilateral interaction has a range of key strategic aspects. First, we get to know the environment and how to operate within it. We get placement and access where our multilateral forces need it. We can leverage the relationships, and importantly we provide an alternative to what the authoritarian states are offering as a future for our partners in the region.

"If we need to respond militarily in the region, we already have a grid and network established. We will have communications networks in place and have exercised mission command. And we have already worked through multilateral formations, so that you have a working C2 model, with all the authorities, in place and an understanding of how you plan, how national authorities affect your planning, how you force project, how you do logistics, and who's going to contribute what to which part of any potential fight."

But he argued that "we are not fit to purpose today to be able to do what we need to do in this strategic space."

We then discussed some aspects of the transition for Army which he envisaged to make the Army "fit for purpose." He highlighted the need to be able to deploy long-range fires in a joint context. We did not discuss how to do this at length, but in my view, it is not simply the ability to fire from the Australian continent or to move first to littoral locations in an Army context. With the emergence of kill web technologies, and third-party targeting, the Army working with Navy and Air Force can shape innovative new ways to cross-target adversarial positions in a variety of new ways going forward, including the use of various robotic or autonomous systems.

Lieutenant General Stuart highlighted the need significantly to enhance the ability of the Army to become mobile in terms of littoral operations. He noted: "We need to be able to thicken our capacity for independent littoral maneuver and also be able to reinforce and disperse our amphibious capability in a meaningful way."

He underscored: "Our 1st Brigade up in Townsville was previously our medium weight brigade. It will now be our core littoral maneuver formation. And this is a capability that our army hasn't had since 1946. And we are building the capability for the brigade to enable us to maneuver in the littorals of our continent and in the region. But it has the capacity for inter-theater, independent intra-theater movement as well. It can also aggregate and disaggregate as part of our amphibious system. We are focused on force dispersal and mobility and providing us with utility to launch a range of different force packages either independently or as part of a combined or multilateral activity."

Lieutenant General Stuart underscored that working with the USMC in terms of the MRF-D rotational force was assisting in this re-design process as well. This means as well a shift in how to organise the Army. He highlighted this aspect as follows: "We've been organized for the wars of the last two decades at the brigade level. We need to move that to the division level to provide the standing headquarters, which are JTFs as well as divisional headquarters and provide our two-star special operations command with the kinds of C2 or C4 capabilities where they can actually command operations in their AORs that incorporate joint and combined agencies. We are organized today on a very much just-in-time efficiency model. We need to be now organized in our warfighting structures that are always on. New and emerging tech, Robotics and Autonomous Systems, Artificial Intelligence and machine learning, quantum and human performance optimization will all have an important impact on our logistics enterprise and in the combat service support space."

As well the modernisation of the Army overall in the new strategic circumstances, we also discussed Army's aviation enterprise and its broader set of challenges. He summarised this thrust towards the future in the following terms: "We are in the cooperative development program for precision strike missiles. We are looking at common effector sets with our navy in the longer term. Our contribution to space and cyber adds significant robustness to the joint effort given we are too small to have separate organizations. And we have completely reoriented our special operations capability along functional lines and are highlighting special warfare and technical enablement to move us away from the focus of the past two decades to what we need to be doing in terms of unconventional warfare and other capabilities to contribute to deterrence in our region."

Lieutenant General Stuart argued for the continued need for armour as well. "We need to modernize that bit of the army that needs to be hardened and protected to be able to guarantee overmatch in time and space and in a distributed way. If you look at it from a full-time brigade formation level in the Australian Army, it's one out of nine formations. "It's not the bulk of the army, but at the end of the day, we'll have about a brigade's worth of armor capability to provide, what we used to call a commander's reserve for those less lethal, less mobile, and less protected formations."

Managing Tradeoffs

Tradeoffs are the name of the game, even if there were to be a future budgetary increase. Only with putting the defence and security challenges in a broader whole of nation context can the kind of challenges facing Australia be dealt with.

The inherent nature of the tradeoff challenge was well articulated by John Conway, the head of Felix Defence and a fellow at the Williams Foundation. As the ADF moves forward, Conway discussed the "triangle of tradeoffs" for development of the force, namely, lethality, survivability, and affordability. It is not about investing in balanced force development for its own sake; rather investments need to be directed to those elements of the ADF which can deliver lethality and survivability at the most affordable cost.

In such a context, advanced training is critical. As he put it: "Within a limited budget, you've now got to think really, really hard about survivability. And you've got to think really hard about preparedness and that links to the training piece. And we've now got an adversary, who is making us spend more and more money on survivability. We'd rather spend money on lethality, but they're making us spend money on survivability because they're becoming increasingly sophisticated, because it's becoming harder and harder to survive. And this is driving up the cost of survivability. But one way of mitigating that risk is getting your training systems right. And being able to fight the best fight with what you've got and invest in warfare rather than just war fighting."[1]

For Conway, the tradeoff between lethality, and survivability is crucial in determining where to put Australia's procurement dollars. In building out the ADF as a joint force, the challenge is to enhance the readiness and capabilities of the current joint force to deliver enhanced capabilities for the direct defence of Australia but at the same time, position the ADF for force modernisation and capability enhancements.

With the reshaping of the ADF as a manoeuvre force operating from the continent and projecting out to Australia's first island chain and beyond (where desired, needed, or appropriate), how then to build out that force going forward? What kind of lethality is needed at what range and with what effect? How to distribute the force effectively and integrate the force to provide the desired lethal effects? How to build out the force within the limits of what manpower, budgets, and society can enable?

Put in other terms, it is not about coming up with a platform shopping list and then going on a shopping spree and simply adding the new stuff to the force. The ADF cannot afford significant disruption to the force as it needs to be able to fight tonight but does need creative innovation driving forward a more lethal and sustainable force going forward.

Not surprisingly, the head of force design for the ADF had especially relevant insights with regard to the trade-off challenge while modernising the force. MAJGEN Anthony Rawlins, head of Force Design, in his presentation to the 28 September 2022 seminar, put the

---

1. For a look at the training dimension, see Robbin Laird, Training for the High-End Fight: The Strategic Shift of the 2020s. 2021.

challenge of building out from the force in being to a more lethal and survivable force precisely in terms of looking beyond major platform buys. He started with a core emphasis on ramping up the capability of the force that has to fight tonight. As he underscored: "Fighting tonight means going with what you have, and what you can feasibly obtain and field in the short term. As a first imperative we need to be immediately and maximally lethal and survivable against a very different potential adversary in the short-term." He then turned to the development of robotic and autonomous systems as force multipliers in the short and medium turn as well as laying a foundation for a shift in the nature of the mission-payload mix in the combat force.

This is how he posed the transition: "Has the hardening of expensive, exquisite, arguably irreplaceable platforms now reached its logical zenith? This is manifest in the arguments for the cheap or the expendable as a supplement or potentially a replacement for expensive crewed platforms going forward. Defence is not just investing in exponential developments in autonomy, artificial intelligence, remote sensing, etc., etc. as an R and D line of effort. But defence is doing so with a view to fielding capability in the immediate short term. And it hardly meets the definition of survivability to be investing in platforms and capabilities that are designed to be expendable."

In this sense, the line between autonomous systems and weapons is a very thin one—the line between a loitering weapon and an autonomous air system when that system is not an expensive UAV but is designed as part of rapid upturn in ISR and C2 capabilities is not very deep.

There is no area where the debate about how to shape force design going forward is more significant to the future of the ADF than the focus on lethality. Although there is a clear commitment to add long range strike weapons like Tomahawk to the force, what role do non-lethal tools play in enhanced lethality against an adversary?

Rawlins put this point very clearly as follows: "What does it mean for a capability to be lethal in a gray zone or a competition environment? Can we describe a capability that is lethal or at least has effects akin to the definition of lethality in the competition or the phase zero environment? Can cyber or other non-kinetic effects be described, and therefore designed going forward through a lethal effects lens?

"There's no doubt that traditionally, we would argue, and we have argued that they contribute to the efficacy or the impact of other lethal effects. But the question now is should we consider them in the same way we have traditionally done with our explosive penetrative weapons sets? I can assure you that this isn't just sophistry for a presentation purpose; it's truly a force design consideration in the contemporary geo-strategic environment. And this is because many now contend that the cyber domain should be treated as another warfighting domain. In fact, this view is gaining increasing traction in other militaries as well as the ADF.

"Many now contend that it's no longer just an enabling domain. Lethal and destructive effects of great significance can be delivered through this domain. And it might be the chosen domain, the first domain through which we seek to do so. But if we look beyond a mortality definition to lethality, into the harmful destructive realm, we're into designing non kinetic capabilities to achieve lethal or highly destructive effects. We already use a very similar targeting methodology in this domain as well as our traditional domains . . . And it's argued by many that greater deterrence at a lesser cost is achieved through investment in these types of capabilities."

If we continue with the discussion of weapons and lethality, how to best design a way ahead from a force design perspective with regard to kinetic weapons? Long-range strike weapons are costly and are imported from the United States even with a ramping up in the short to midterm of Australian capabilities to participate in a broader arsenal of democracy with allies. What mix of weapons can be built going forward? What targeting options does Australia need?

If there is no desire or need to strike Chinese territory directly (as China is a nuclear power), how best to strike Chinese forces to get the kind of crisis management and combat effect desired? Can Australia build a more cost-effective mix of weapons than the United States currently possesses? How to develop partnerships with other allies to do so? How to manage the inevitable conflicts among allies when priorities are dictated by national survival rather than by working together?

At the seminar, the most comprehensive discussion of the challenges facing Australia in shaping a way ahead for the weapons enterprise was provided by Dr. Andrew Dowse, director, RAND Australia. This is what he argued: "Weapon demands might be assessed in terms of conflict intensity and conflict duration. In any substantial conflict, it's likely that our stocks of exquisite weapons would be quickly consumed.

"Even if supply routes remain open, we should not be too confident of resupply for two reasons. First, high intensity conflict will also most likely involve our U.S. allies, the source of most of our weapons. This raises the prospect of divergent allied priorities.

"Second, weapons manufacturing over the years has been rationalized to peacetime efficiencies, with limitations on the global ability to surge production. So typically, the high-end weapons that we need to fight need to be held in inventory." He then went on to argue that targeting tradeoffs on high-end weapons underscored the need to shape a broader weapons arsenal. "In any conflict, there will be tension in targeting processes between the use of such weapons early in conflict, and ensuring some capabilities are held in reserve. It will be important that the replenishment of weapons during protracted conflict keeps pace with demand.

"Thus, it may be reasonable to prioritize domestic production of explosive ordnance and low-end weapons that can be supplied in operationally relevant timelines. In developing priorities for inventory and domestic production, which might be somewhat aligned to demands of initial and protracted conflict, respectively, we should consider the value of affordable mass weapons, especially if they might be replenished at a rate that matches demand. This quality through quantity approach is increasingly being facilitated through technological development, which provides greater precision for less cost. It is a concept that can be applied to employment of multiple weapons against high value targets, including use of asymmetry to simultaneously use dissimilar weapons. It is also a concept that is relevant to our platforms with dispersion and integration of force elements, enhancing collective lethality and survivability, at the same time, reducing the impact of the attrition of our own force.

"Hence, it may be opportune for the ADF to pursue smaller platforms and greater use of network uncrewed systems. And such a concept of reducing the concentration of our force is one that can be extended to passive defence as a significant risk for Australia is that of a pre-emptive attack.

"Thus, measures of hardening redundancy, dispersion and disaggregation are critical to ensure that we don't suffer attrition at the beginning of conflict. And this is not only about the physical domains, but also about protecting systems in the cyber domain."

In short, force design considerations built out from the reworking of how best to deploy, operate, and sustain the current force, and in doing so, it is possible identify critical gaps which can realistically can be filled in the short to midterm. Enhancing lethality through working an integrated lethal and non-lethal offensive strike force is a high priority. Leveraging automated systems for appropriate mission sets is a key part of enhancing both mass and reducing the challenge of survivability; when designed to be attributable, survivability is not the dominant consideration for that part of the force.

Crafting a Way Ahead

In reshaping the ADF and the defence ecosystem in Australia to deal with the direct threats to Australia posed in the Indo-Pacific, a much broader focus is required than simply on the ADF and its role as a professional force. The ADF is professional and capable, but it is small. And it relies on a civilian infrastructure which is fairly limited as well.

But when one focuses on ways to ramp up the capabilities of the force, this will not come with simply buying shiny new platforms. As one redesigns and reshapes the force with increased numbers of personnel, training is a key part of the effort.

And to manage disruptions as one looks in the near to midterm to add new force enablers, such as robotic systems, is a challenge to be dealt with as well. The ADF needs to be able to fight in the near term which means that the Australian government cannot simply just reorganise the force to the point of reducing operational capabilities. What is required in the shift to the priority in the direct defence of Australia is a degree of honesty about alliances, partnerships, and vulnerabilities in terms of mobilisation potential for Australia on its own. Australia cannot only depend on an ally to show up and protect its interests. It cannot assume that it can engage in extended defence with the existing level of defence supplies or the currently extant defence ecosystem for sustained operations in the near term.

What Australia needs to be able to do is not only to project power in its region, but to do so with as much resilient strategic depth as it can muster with an alliance effort with the allies on the same page regarding the objectives for crisis management.

Chapter Four

Australia and the Arsenal of Democracy

With the shift from a primary focus on the away game to the direct defence of Australia, the broader focus on defence and security needs to move from warfighting to war. Or put in other words, the ADF has been focused on the evolution of capabilities for warfighting while working with allies in the Middle East land wars but is now focused on building defence in depth for Australia in its region. Both efforts entail working effectively with allies; but in the land wars case, the ADF was part of a broader allied logistics and sustainment effort with just in time logistics being sufficient. In the direct defence of Australia case, how to work with allies and with whom in what specific circumstances and to be able to ensure that Australia's priorities have more than a seat at the table is a work in progress.

Because the challenge posed by the twenty-first-century authoritarians, notably China, has a direct impact on the entire paradigm in which Australia has thrived economically and globally, the entire gamut of economic, political, cultural, informational, and global trade relationships are involved now in the broader whole of government and whole of nation effort to ensure the survival of Australia as a liberal democratic nation in a congenial global order.

One of the most direct statements of the intersection between the ADF and the nation was made by the Chief of Navy, Vice Admiral Mark Hammond. This is how he put it in his presentation to the Williams Foundation seminar on September 28, 2022: "I believe it's important to raise our eyes above the tactical level for a moment to reflect on why we build and employ an integrated force. And I say this because what we build and what we do with it matters only in so much as it enhances our national well-being.

"Our national well-being like all nations is derived from sustained economic prosperity, and peaceful coexistence with nations. And as a trading island nation connected to the global trading system by seabed cables, and maritime commerce, our economic well-being is almost exclusively enabled by the sea and by the seabed.

"Enablement though is not enough. Sustained economic prosperity has only been possible because these systems—freedom of navigation for commerce, and seabed infrastructure which enables our financial and strategic connectivity with the global trading system—have flourished in an environment of acceptance and adherence to the complex array of treaties, laws, and conventions that for almost 80 years have been iterated, improved and almost universally supported. We call this the rules-based order, and we credit it with providing good order at sea in the collective interest of peace for all nations. Those of us who understand Australia derives its well-being from this system are alarmed that such norms are being challenged.

"We are concerned that the right to peaceful coexistence with other nations can no longer be assumed. As former minister for defence, the Honorable Kim Beazley stated in Perth last month, and I paraphrase, what right do we have to exist as a sovereign nation of only 25 million people occupying an island continent with room and natural resources the envy of the world?

"The answer is the rights conferred by adherence to the rules-based order. The very rights we have assumed to be enduring and beyond contest for decades. But that is no longer the case. This system is now being challenged and our government has commissioned the defence strategic review in response to these challenges.

"It is reasonable to conclude that that which cannot be assumed, must be guaranteed. And that is why the lethality and survivability of our defence forces is being re-examined. In this context, there is a direct and distinct nexus between the lethality and survivability of the integrated force and the survivability of our nation. And this relationship is recognized by our prime minister in the last month. The Honorable Anthony Albanese has stated that he sees the three key principles of our current security policy are to defend our territorial integrity, to protect our political sovereignty from external pressure and to promote Australia's economic prosperity through a strong economy and resilient supply chains . . . Australia is a paradox. The geography which makes it difficult to invade and conquer Australia also makes Australia dependent upon seaborne trade. In other words, Australia might not be vulnerable to invasion, but the hostile power does not need to invade Australia to defeat Australia."

Unpacking an understanding of the evolving relationship between the nation and the ADF is at the heart of reworking the defence of the nation in the years to come. The defence capabilities which have enabled the ADF to deliver significant but targeted warfighting capability will now be adapted and refocused on Australia's direct defence and role in its region.

How will the necessary ADF mobilisation potential intersect with the mobilisation of the nation? How will the ADF build out its workforce and be supported by the enhanced capability of domestic defence industry to support the ADF in a crisis or sustained conflict?

The Challenge of Funding a Relevant Defence Effort

Let us return to John Conway of Felix Defence and his treatment of the tradeoffs challenge. In our discussion with him, Conway has underscored the "triangle of tradeoffs" for development of the force, namely, lethality, survivability, and affordability. It is not about investing in balanced force development for its own sake; rather investments need to be directed to those elements of the ADF which can deliver lethality and survivability at the most affordable cost.

We focused the discussion on the challenges of enhanced investment in survivability prioritizing investments in the lethality of the force, and the overall challenge of affordability due to the general global economic situation affecting the liberal democracies. This is how Conway put it: "I think we're seeing now an increasing number of unknowns, particularly regarding the business and economics of defence, not just in Australia, but globally, where the impact of a potentially deep-seated recession across all of the Western nations is underway.

"A number of risks—supply chain shortfalls, exchange rate fluctuations, fuel costs and others—translate into higher costs, in particular for sustainment. And while the general metrics for measuring defence budgets is a percentage of GDP, and with GDP shrinking, then obviously a percentage of GDP yields less money for defence.

"There's a clear limit to that overall bucket of money available. And if through the global economic situation, we have to spend proportionately much more of our money on sustainment and training, and in the re-posturing of our force such as with regard to basing and mobility, it leaves less money available to acquire new technology and the new platforms which are necessary to give us a lethality edge. What we are going to see across all Western defence forces for the foreseeable future is increasing costs through sustainment and force development. This means that less money will be available to buy the new technology and the platforms that the services require in an environment where the threat is dictating a change in our force structure.

"With the money getting tighter and at the same time the threat becoming more demanding, it will be much harder for the ADF to do the things that government might want us to do. One obvious area of investment over and above new platforms is therefore training or more specifically mission rehearsal. Increasing capability by investing in training systems through existing sustainment contracts would be a great quick way of improving both survivability and lethality."

Conway also argued for the importance for the business sector, and not just those labelled defence companies, to work new relationships with the government to be able to deliver the right capabilities for an affordable cost and be part of an overall national effort for enhanced national resilience in the region, especially for force posture initiatives.

This is how he put it: "We need to find innovative ways of bringing money into defence and ways to bring a wider range of industry into the broader social and national defence enterprise so that we can continue to invest in new technology as well as the sustainment systems. The pandemic plus the knock-on consequences of Ukraine are driving significant pressures in how we do defence and fund defence. The way the trends are going at the moment with affordability and survivability, they are not acting in our favor. They're working against us."

Conway underscored that notably in the basing, sustainment, and stockpiling of capabilities areas, there was a clear need to rethink the template of how defence forces are supported and funded. "How do we incentivize defence industry to come up with smart answers especially regarding force posture changes? Because they've historically been excellent at responding to market conditions to innovate and to make things happen. There's a responsibility on defence industry's shoulders now to get out front of the problem and start coming up with ideas rather than simply saying, we need to buy more of something, and we need to buy a depot to store it in.

"There has to be a smarter way of doing that, which incentivizes industry, but at the same time provides defence with the mission assurance it requires from its supply chains. And we need to unlock market power in another sense, namely allowing companies coming from outside of traditional defence background to bring in new ideas about the development of our critical supply chains, through trusted partnerships rather than simply relying on legacy global supply chains. We need to start looking outside of defence for new ideas and be more welcoming of new partnerships to deliver the sustainment enterprise we need. We need to break outside our bubble and stop trying to sort the problem out from a narrowly defined legacy defence family.

"In spite of the deep challenges, we need to have a winning mindset. Part of achieving this result is that we need to unlock the power of the private sector and be more open minded about how we manage risk within defence."

The Stockpiling Challenge as Part of Resilience

When one considers how Australia will build defence resilience, a key place to start is the question of the shift from just in time logistics to how best to provide for stockpiles of critical war materials. When engaged in warfighting for the past twenty years, the liberal democracies used a just in time logistics approach. The American systems used by the ADF have been delivered by either military or commercial means from a peacetime production or sustainment production line.

But the war in Ukraine has exposed the weakness of these systems and the need to build a realistic but new approach to the arsenal of democracy. How does one build an arsenal of democracy essentially from economies which are service oriented and increasingly focused on "green" production? How do you build stockpiles of relevant war materials, when there are no policy focuses on what is essential? Where do you stockpile war materials? How do you move them where you need to in a time of crisis so that they are survivable until used?

There is clear tradeoff between stockpiling and investing in new systems. Potential for prevailing in a major crisis or war is different from adding a new system for enhanced potential warfighting gains. Indeed, that is why the last time the United States had a director for mobilisation in DOD was in the Reagan Administration. By the way, this person was none other than my frequent co-author the Honorable Ed Timperlake.

The production of relevant stockpiles could be aided by an approach where major allies cooperate in Australia in building enhanced military capability from Northern or Western Australia. But even if allies began to operate more from Australian territory, would they combine this effort with enhanced stockpiling of supplies? Who would guard them? Who would move them in times of crisis to areas of optimal use?

There are new ways to provide support, such as 3D printing or robotics in logistical support, but the shift towards production of more war material to prepare for war is not a current budgetary priority for the liberal democracies.   It is also the case that commercial systems modified for military use have not been fully exploited to allow for crisis use of those systems to bolster availability of that military system in a crisis. The 737 is the case in point. Even though the 737 platform is used for the Wedgetail and the P-8, neither program has been managed with a core consideration of how to support the fleet with commercial parts—even though often the same parts!

In a 2022 interview with Colonel David Beaumont, we discussed the challenge for Australia to sustain the force for the time needed to prevail in conflict or crisis management. This is how he put it: "The belligerent who can respond quickest and can return to support the combat force will be the one that emerges and has the greatest chance for success."

The next phase of ADF development will be built around the direct defence of Australia and its ability to operate within its core defence perimeter with an integrated but distributed force, and its ability to mobilise a sustainment system for operations, but that will only occur with the broader capability of the Australian nation to mobilise as well. Mobilisation is not simply an ADF concept, but it is a whole of nation commitment.

This is how Beaumont put it in our conversation: "We need to go beyond simply discussing ADF mobilization in a crisis. We need to understand what the limits and constraints are on what the ADF can do for itself and what might it need from the nation. This will help us understand exactly what capabilities or support mechanisms need to be built within the ADF, or what policies and plans may be required to help govern national responses to a crisis."

What Role for Australian Defence Industry?

By outsourcing industry to its main competitor—China—Australia and its allies have outsourced the industrial production central to having an arsenal of democracy in times of conflict. How then might Australia and its allies and partners build or rebuild an arsenal of democracy?

Clearly, one consideration is to expand what the Australian defence industry can provide locally in a crisis. But it is important to be realistic about what can be achieved domestically. We will consider the case of weapons provided to the ADF in a crisis by various approaches, including building local defence industrial capabilities. But here we will reflect on how to realistically consider the nature of the problem.

In a 2022 interview, Matthew Wilson, the CEO of Penten, discussed the role of the Australian defence industry in direct defence of Australia. The interview focused largely on his assessment of the digital defence and security domain because logically that is where its business operates. We started with a discussion of the core book which analysed the contribution of the U.S. industry in winning World War II. *Forge of Democracy* laid the conditions under which the government worked with the industry to create an arsenal of democracy.

As Wilson noted: "The book provides a look at what is required to mobilize an industrial base. What financial incentives are required? What approach by government is required to mobilize such a defence industrial base? If industry is to make smart investments to help build and support an arsenal of democracy, how to do so?"

And shaping an arsenal of democracy either starts with or includes securing the digital domain. Here Wilson argued that Australia is making strides in the right direction. "It's taken us a little while to try and get norms of behavior established concerning what's acceptable and what's not acceptable within the cyber realm. But one of the things I'm actually quite proud of from Australian perspective is that Australia—both government and industry—has accepted the need to support the policy development in that space."

Wilson noted that such an effort is crucial to operating in the "grey zone of conflict" which Australia operates within with China and others. "But now the challenge is changing. The truth of matter is, the last 20 years, we've been in conflicts that we haven't needed to consider the interruption of the digital supply lines as a core defence and security challenge: it was not going to happen, and it didn't happen. Now it is a core element for the defence and security of the Commonwealth."

"And in this domain, we have to think not only about the first strike. It's about what a sustained conflict looks like in the digital domain."

Wilson assessed the challenge as follows: "When you think about cyber resilience for us, it is slightly different to the way that China has to think about cyber resilience. Because China would rely on their actual industrial base to produce the material to be able to fight effectively."

Such defence material will exist only in the alliance team concept for Australia. "We're on a team, and you need to make a contribution to the team; you've got to pick your places where we can make those types of contributions. My genuine belief is that this is a space where

Australia can create some industrial capability that it can feed back into the allied combined effort to create an arsenal of democracy."

Wilson felt that there was a need for a comprehensive approach to thinking about a way ahead for the arsenal of democracy. "We need to think of how we can mobilize industry and not just the defence industry narrowly considered."

In other words, Australia needs to provide for core capabilities such as digital defence, but in an alliance context. Now let us now consider the case of munitions and weapons.

The Weapons Case

One should start first with the question of industrial age versus new industrial age weapons. For example, how important to core capabilities such as artillery shells remain to a defense arsenal? And innovations that we are seeing with artillery in working new con-ops (shoot and scoot) and with radars to work dispersed artillery to defend against drones or to work with them for new targeting solutions could well see an expanded role for artillery in the period ahead.

Artillery pieces can operate on land or be used on ships as part of kill box control approaches as well. And systems like HIMRS are playing an increasing role in firepower for ground base forces whether at home or deployed on expeditionary bases.

But prior to getting esoteric about the future of new weapons, building a strong domestic capability for artillery-based weapons is a key requirement for a secure weapons base in Australia, which currently is very thin as well.

And in the weapons area, it is especially important to pay heed to the chief of army's warning: "There is a prevailing commentary today that speaks with undue precision and certainty about the 'next war.' It generally comes from a perspective that focuses exclusively on the changing character of war, which either dismisses or ignores its enduring nature.

"It discounts the effects of fog, friction, chaos, and individual agency on the course of a war. It describes a symmetrical response in a single modality of warfare. It supposes will can be imposed and can be resisted at ever increasing distance and without having to close with an adversary.

"It focuses on the outcome of the first battle or battles rather than the war. It imagines that the next war will be short, decisive, and clean. And it confuses targeting and tactics for operational art and strategy. Unfortunately, history, including Australia's history, does not support these hypotheses."

If we go next to the stated desire to have weapons which can strike at a distance which would affect Chinese behaviour in a crisis, we enter a terrain where consideration of range of a weapon needs to be balanced with the ability of platforms to work sensor-shooter relationships at distance or kill web considerations.

The establishment of Australian Missile Corporation has been done with a keen concern on obtaining longer range weapons for Australia. The acquisition of TLAMS for RAN ships is a start, and the central role of Lockheed Martin and Raytheon in such systems certainly justifies their role in establishing an Australian sovereign guided weapons enterprise.

But this is a pump-priming exercise. What would come next?

The United States along with its allies have not invested in long-range strike missiles. One reason the Trump Administration withdrew from the INF treaty was to do so. After all, China is leading the way in building such weapons. It is important for Australia to build such missiles, especially a land-based variant with other allies.

Could Australia develop with allies a modular range of land-based missiles useful to provide domestically built and supported capability?

Could they follow a Kongsberg model in working with the United States or other allies in the development of modular land-based strike missiles? Here, Australia could use its territory to advantage along with forward operating air and sea systems which could identify dynamic targets for the land-based systems.

The Kongsberg model refers to the build of the naval strike missile (NSM) and joint strike missile (JSM) by the Norwegian company. The NSM has been adopted by a wide range of allies as well; the entire family of missiles can be seen to be significant contributors to the arsenal of democracy. Currently, there are nine customers for the NSM: Norway, Poland, Malaysia, Germany, United States (for both the U.S. Navy and USMC), Romania, Canada, Spain, and Australia. When I was in Poland in 2021, I talked with the Polish military about their use of a truck-mounted version of the NSM which they moved to various points of interest to Poland, much as the Marines are now doing with their approach to mobile basing in support of the US Navy.

And the agreement with Raytheon has meant that the Kongsberg missile has an additional assembly capability located in the United States which can generate a ramp up in production as well. And this historical partnership based in the NASAMS has allowed the two companies to shape innovative ways to work together in the common allied interests, such as the evolution of the capability of the NASAMS system.

The JSM is in development and close to deployment by the world's F-35 forces. The NSM becoming transfigured into the JSM meant modifications to fit the internal bay of the F-35. It has a longer range than the NSM dependent on flight profile. It has two-way communications capability which allows it to be used in a wolfpack concept of operations or retargeted in flight by a designated third party, which could include an ally as well. Initial users of the missile will be Japan and Norway, with the United States, the United Kingdom, Australia, and South Korea likely as early adapters for their F-35s as well.

The JSM can be launched from a variety of sea-borne, land, or air platforms. And it is a kill web weapon, in that it can be re-targeted in flight by a third-party system, such as an airborne command post. Abort mission and retargeting aspects of NSM is taken into account by the use of target matching capabilities combined with a wide field of view seeker imaging target sensor. In a kill-web context, the NSM is a rapid deployable effector that can respond to both naval and land target sets based upon third-party ISR resources in the web.

But the simple point is that the missile is being widely used by many allies and can be used by a diversity of platforms. In an interview at the Euronaval exhibition held during the week of October 16, 2022, there was a chance to talk about the NSM with Stein Engen, regional sales director, Kongsberg Strike Missiles. Engen started by discussing the origin of the NSM.

"The threat scenario in developing the missile has always been the Russian Navy. We have a small navy and air force, so we needed a highly accurate and capable missile to replace the Penguin. As the missile developed and then was deployed by our navy, and its ability to be used against both land and sea targets became recognized by other navies to be a market leader. The evaluations made by the U.S. Navy and other allied navies underscored that NSM is a cost-efficient weapon because of its accuracy and ability to get to the desired target, even in contested area, and to deliver its effects even against well defended strategic target sets. The advanced target matching capabilities of the NSM IR seeker enables strike against prioritized targets and also avoid hitting unintentional targets and civilian shipping."

And missiles like the NSM and JSM represent payloads to missions as key capability. With the flexibility of launch point coupled with the flexibility in the decision of where the inflight missile needs to target, these are very capable kill-web weapons.

And as allies share commonality in the missile base, not only can you build up stockpiles, but you can also exercise shared use of these weapons in dealing with the adversary in situations where the allies are operating as a distributed force but seeking integrated effects from the coalition operation. In other words, the capability represented in NSM and JSM can be seen to a key part of the wider effort to ensure that there is a viable "arsenal of democracy."

It could be argued that the most immediate way to enhance the population of longer-range strike capabilities would be to build out systems in numbers and capabilities. A forward operating air force with longer range weapons has credible punch, notably if directed by a fifth-generation force. That force packs punch with the range of missiles it holds itself or can target acquire and fire from another platform or location.

The mistake made repeatedly by those who think in legacy terms about the F-35 is to confuse its weapon's role with what itself carries on board. It is a kill-web platform which identifies targets for the weapons deployed by others. Could these weapons be land-based? Could they be based on an arsenal ship? Or an arsenal plane?

For example, one could use an airlifter as a weapons carrier even if one later decided to buy a bomber. One would get use of the air-lifter in its many missions but also use it in case of need to ramp up the deployed arsenal. Dougal Robertson and Chris McInnes of Felix Defence have argued the case that the quickest way to add range and lethality to the ADF is by building a larger air force. They argue that the RAAF's aircraft and weapons have better range and responsiveness than any proposed alternatives. Not surprisingly, their argument is based in part on the fact that the RAAF is adding enhanced range missiles to the fleet, and by adding additional tanker support, one pushes the force further and operates longer from Australian shores.

They argued: "The RAAF will have two important long-range anti-shipping and land attack weapons in the inventory by 2025. They are the 500-km-plus Long-Range Anti-Shipping Missile (LRASM) and the 900-km plus Joint Air to Surface Standoff Missile–Extended Range (JASSM-ER), both carrying 450-kg warheads ideal for large targets. The RAAF's F/A-18F Super Hornets will initially carry these weapons and, depending on loadout and aerial refuelling support, can fly at least 1,500 km (and return). This means a weapon effectiveness radius of at least 2,000 km against ships and nearly 2,500 km for land strike.

"A RAAF 'strike package' taking off from Darwin can reach the southern Philippines, the Java Sea and the Bismarck Sea. From Townsville, the seas around the Solomon Islands are covered, including all the Coral Sea. Aircraft operating from Learmonth, near Exmouth in Western Australia, could strike ships trying to break through chokepoints at the Sunda Strait (west of Java) and the Lombok Strait (east of Bali). It would take less than three hours from aircraft launch for weapons to impact their targets.

"Aircraft can then relocate from base to base, hitting land or maritime targets across an area larger than the entire European continent (10.1 million square kilometres). Versatile platforms like the Super Hornet can fly multiple mission types, so RAAF strike forces could locate and destroy land targets to Australia's east on Tuesday, enemy shipping in the Sunda Strait on Wednesday, then mount an airborne defence of Darwin on Thursday.

"These missions would all be launched from mainland Australia—meaning no need for potentially provocative pre-positioning, negotiating base permissions with regional partners, or defending deployed forces and supply lines. If forward bases are available, the RAAF's reach gets longer."[1]

In addition, there are a number of technologies in process which change the weapons calculus. The impact of this on Australian industry is the need to enhance its involvement in the adjacent technologies affecting weaponization as well as the areas directly involved ensuring that there is a sufficient weapons arsenal for the ADF. To be cutting edge without real capabilities will ensure that the edge you are on is the nation's survival.

What are some of the dynamics affecting a rethink of weaponization? First, there is the arrival of directed energy weapons, notably first on capital ships. The reason directed energy weapons are to be operationally on capital ships is simply because these weapons require significant power and cooling to work. As they appear on American navy capital ships, the most logical ship in the RAN to have this capability would be the new Hunter Class frigate.

This would then affect deployment options. Obviously, directed energy weapons provide a cost-effective way to weaponize the platform they are on. As the power generated grows, the weapon can provide support for ashore assets, whether Army or air force. Directed energy weapons aboard capital ships could provide defence capabilities for agile combat employment for the RAAF, dependent on where the mobile base is located.

---

1. https://adbr.com.au/the-quickest-way-to-more-range-and-letha
   lity-for-the-adf-is-a-bigger-air-force/

Second, there is the dynamic relationship of robotic to manned systems. Guided weapons are unmanned systems; maritime autonomous systems and airborne autonomous systems are also unmanned; how well they operate together?

A case in point is the Australian loyal wingman. In an article by Bradley Perrett published on 16 December 2021, this how the loyal wingman could provide kinetic support to a maned fighter: "An ATS (airpower training system or the loyal wingman) could attack much as any other fast jet would, releasing bombs while approaching the target and turning away as they flew onward. If the drone knew its position precisely enough at the point of bomb release, inertial guidance in the weapons might alone be good enough for hitting the target. For use against ground vehicles, the ATS would need an electro-optical and infrared sensor in its nose to detect and classify them. Once launched in their general direction, a bomb could again detect and classify them, requiring no more support from the aircraft. But adding a laser designator in the ATS's nose would give the aircraft greater control. For the operating air force, such capabilities against relatively easy targets would release crewed fighters for more difficult missions. A force of loyal wingmen with these capabilities would also enable more targets to be attacked over a given period of time. This would debilitate the enemy faster and stress its air-surveillance and fighter capacity."[2]

Another example of uncrewed systems which could provide weapons support is that the U.S. Navy is looking at the possibility of light surface torpedoes aboard a twelve-foot UAS as the wingman for its mothership. Indeed, the entire concept of a mothership is being created from the emergence of uncrewed systems in support of the

---

2. https://www.aspistrategist.org.au/loyal-wingmen-could-be-use d-to-break-open-enemy-defences/

ship. They will function first in terms of operating initially as extended sensor reach but then providing additional lethal weapons augmentation will not far behind.

In short, weapons provision will be part of rebuilding the arsenal of democracy. The initial effort could focus on the "industrial" age weapons in short supply, short term gap fillers (TLAMS), and enhanced range weapons for the air force.

But what is next? What is feasible? How to work the allied environment? And will Australia do like Norway and focus on a key aspect of its strategic environment in building out its weapon capacity? Might that be leveraging innovations with like-minded allies on land-based systems? Or might that be in working with like positioned allies with manpower shortages on using uncrewed systems as force extenders?

An example of this second approach was provided by Marcus Hellyer in his treatment of Australia within an allied arsenal of democracy. As he argued in an article published on 25 August 2022: "The basic fact is that defence is an artificially protected monopoly. Monopolies simply can't innovate rapidly. The reason our electricity sector has managed to move down the path of renewables as far as it has despite the stonewalling of the previous federal government and the incumbent major players is that many other players have gained entry, creating competition and driving innovation. There are ways in which defence should enjoy a natural monopoly; we don't advocate for mercenaries.

"But when defence is both a monopoly provider of security services to the government and a monopsony consumer of security goods and services from industry, it is a recipe for stagnation. Sometimes defence needs firm external direction—it's the role of the new government and the defence strategic review to provide that. Developing Australian companies' ability to produce small-guided weapons at scale won't just benefit our defence force. We've recently seen the prospects for conflict over Taiwan intensify, provoking greater debate in Australia about what we would do if Beijing ordered an assault.

"Providing Taiwan with tens of thousands of small kamikaze drones that can sink landing craft and destroy armoured vehicles will make a tangible difference to its prospects of resisting invasion—perhaps even more of a difference than sending a small number of high-value Australian Defence Force assets and their crews. By leveraging the benefits of Industry 4.0, Australia can become a key part of the arsenal of democracy."[3]

Robotics and AI

During a major speech in early November 2022, Navy Admiral Charles A. Richard, commander of U.S. Strategic Command issued this warning concerning the pace of development of U.S. forces compared to China: "We used to know how to move fast, and we have lost the art of that . . . We have got to get back into the business of not talking about how we are going to mitigate our assumed eventual failure to get Columbia in on time, and B-21, and LRSO, and flip it to the way we used to ask questions in this nation, which is what's it going to take? Is it money? Is it people? Do you need authorities? What risk? That's how we got to the Moon by 1969. We need to bring

---

3. https://www.aspistrategist.org.au/australia-can-be-an-arsenal-of
-democracy/

some of that back. Otherwise, China is simply going to out-compete us, and Russia isn't going anywhere anytime soon."[4]

Given the importance of speed to deployment of new capabilities which Australia suffers as well, how to ramp up a more rapid capability development to deployment process?

A clear emphasis has been emerging within Australia to do so by leveraging robotics and artificial intelligence capabilities. But how to do so? And within the force, where can this be done? Where can autonomous systems be used in the near term to augment the ISR, C2, and lethal and non-lethal capabilities of the ADF? Can innovative ways to operate modular task forces including such systems be included?

Inherent in such an effort is the possibility as well of attenuating the manpower shortage for the combat force as well as for mobilising civilians in support of the nation. For example, at the Williams Foundation seminar on Next Generation Autonomous Systems on April 8, 2021, a key focus was on how the ADF could leverage a broader ecosystem of change in the commercial sector where robotics and artificial intelligence were playing key roles.

The presentation at the seminar by Professor Jason Scholz, CEO of the Trusted Autonomous Systems Defence Cooperation Centre focused on this challenge. This is how Scholz described the challenge and the way ahead for the ADF in the autonomous systems area: "Autonomous systems for air, land, sea, space, cyber, electromagnetic, and information environments offers huge potential to enhance Australia's critical and scarce manned platforms and soldiers, and realizing

---

4. https://www.defense.gov/News/News-Stories/Article/Article/3209416/stratcom-commander-says-us-should-look-to-1950s-to-regain-competitive-edge/

this now and into the future requires leadership in defence, in industry, in science and technology and academia with an ambition and an appetite for risk in effecting high-impact and disruptive change."

He underscored the crucial importance of leveraging the broader commercial developments and uses already underway. "We need a diversity of means to make this work. And it happened into the future. This is an initiative of defence and Defence Science and Technology (DST) group. It leverages strong commercial technology drivers to solve these long-term challenges experienced by the department."

According to the head of maritime autonomous systems in the Royal Australian Navy, Commodore Darron Kavanagh underscored: "As soon as I say I've got requirements for a combat system, I immediately go into a classical systems engineering approach. But that approach doesn't actually allow for the agility necessary rapidly to change that combat system. If I look at classical primes, they are often hardware first companies, software second. And there's a lot of legacy in the design. One of the things we've been looking at is how would you take a software first approach to accelerate our maritime autonomous systems capabilities. This is one of the reasons that the sovereign industry players that we've selected recently to work with in the autonomous systems areas are software-driven in their development rather than platform-focused."

But with a focus on kill-web operational concepts, the emphasis is upon the effective operation of a distributed force where payloads to missions is a key element of building the modular task forces at the tactical edge which form the combat nodes from which force integration can be built in a fluid combat situation. Maritime autonomous systems are defined by the payloads and the software which enable those payloads to support the missions in the distributed battlespace, rather than by the platforms which hold them.

This is a very different way around from the legacy approach to platform prioritisation and platform development. While certainly, core air, sea, and ground platforms built under evolving systems engineering models will remain a key element of force design and development, the path for maritime autonomous systems is significantly different.

The ADF has been looking for some time to work rapid software development and insertion into combat forces. This is much harder to do with core platforms than with software-driven, payload-defined, maritime autonomous systems. This is why a key contribution to the ADF as a joint force can be provided by the kind of acquisition and operational models being shaped around maritime autonomous systems.

These systems do not follow a classical understanding of product development. While the approach does develop prototypes: this is not the primary focus. It is about focusing on operational effects: as both contributions to the force in being and continuous and ongoing experimentation for force development under actual operational conditions.

As Darron Kavanagh underscored in my 2022 interview with him : "If you actually want to deliver something different, if you want to actually get what I'd call asymmetric war fighting effects, then you must be prepared to experiment. Because those concepts of operations are not going to come from replacing what you have. Or indeed, an incremental improvement of what you have. You actually have to leverage what the technology will give you. It is because less and less it's about a platform. It's more and more about your intent. So, that's command-and-control, and the payloads that deliver that intent."

Commodore Darron Kavanagh underscored that the ADF is evolving and building out an ADF capable of effective distributed operations. And maritime autonomous systems will be a key enabler for such operations. To do so, the systems need to be operating in the force as part of the overall operational capability for the force. As the ADF gains experience with these systems, they will face ongoing development and experimentation, both in terms of the payloads they carry as well as the operating systems on the platforms, as well as seeing platform development to better enable payload performance and targeted relevance to the operating force.

As Kavanagh put it: "The challenge is being able to field them at the speed of relevance. That is the difficulty in a bureaucracy such as any military. And so, one of the reasons it's important to spend that time to work out how do we constructively disrupt? We are not building a one-off system. The focus is upon delivering asymmetric warfighting effects again and again."

Commodore Kavanagh emphasised that the terminology is important in understanding what maritime autonomous systems are and how their role within the operational force will grow over time. "I refer to these systems as uncrewed systems. And the reason I use that term is that it is less and less about the vehicle that actually delivers the effect. The payload is really important as it could be on all sorts of different vehicles, whether it's in the air, below, in certain circumstances, or on the surface. This requires you thinking in a different way about how do you plug and fight different elements into the combat force."

There is clear promise in this approach and a key element in jump starting a more rapid use of technology operations approach. Such an approach could be facilitated as well by changes in how training of the combat forces intersects with the development of capabilities for use.

The Australian Defence Force has set a tough bar for itself—shaping an integrated force and crafting an ability to design such a force. This is a tough bar but one which they are trying to energise in part by leveraging their new platforms to shape a way ahead beyond the classic after-market integration strategy.

But how best to do this with regard to training and development of the force? And how to maximise the combat effectiveness to be achieved rather than simply connecting platforms without a significant combat effect?

The Limits and Opportunities for the Australian Industry

Alan Dupont has argued that "Our vulnerability to supply-chain disruptions and the weakness of our defence industrial base could be fatal in a time of rising conflict and heightened geopolitical risk. On the opportunity side, a robust, export-generating defence industry can help provide the jobs and smart skills that Anthony Albanese says he wants." He noted that "We still import most of our major defence equipment. Our naval shipbuilding industry is in disarray. Australian companies are bit players in a defence industry dominated by big overseas prime contractors. And we have no defence industry strategic plan or a funding model that meets our needs and provides a pathway to greater defence self-reliance. Israel and Sweden, both smaller than us, have built world-class defence industries."

So, the question in the weapons area must be: What is the domain of the possible for the Australian defence industry in the weapons area?

A number of approaches are possible. But realistic approaches need to be shaped which clearly recognise the manpower, financial, development, and related constraints facing any notion of complete Australian sovereignty in this area.

The first is to build industrial age ammunition capabilities and to work with allied nations who are innovating in the innovative use and development of land-based systems designed in part to defeat and work with drone systems.

The second is to shape industrial capabilities to develop and build land-based missile capabilities with allies who have a similar need.

The third is to shape robust industrial capacity to work with allies in the key areas associated with the evolution of weapons technologies, sensors, robotics, and directed energy weapons, and to position the Australian industry to be able to produce key elements for the allied weapons enterprise, and where possible, to co-produce the weapons themselves.

The testing territory which Australia possesses is the key asset to leverage in shaping a way ahead in any allied arsenal of democracy. Years ago, when I first visited Australia and before the Obama Administration choked off research on hypersonic weapons, this was already evident.

This is what I wrote in 2014:

The opportunity is to shape convergent modernisation to the benefit of the allies and the United States to deal with the challenges from China and North Korea. It is not us versus the Chinese; it is the allied engagement shaping deterrence in depth against a China with no strategic allies, other than Russia and North Korea.

Recent Chinese tests on hypersonics have underscored that several countries are working to be able to build operational hypersonics platforms, for a variety of purposes. You wouldn't want to be second to the table with a hypersonic strike missile. Partnering with a solid ally like Australia can help ensure that does not happen to the United States. But this requires significant commitment to steady investment in the hypersonics research area.

Australia has a small but cutting-edge team of hypersonic researchers, with the test ranges to play out the evolving technologies, and with significant global working relationships. Research in this field can clearly yield possible capabilities for space access as well, with an ability to launch rapidly ISR and C2 capabilities for Australia and as part of the effort to overcome the tyranny of distance to deal with longer-range threats and challenges as well.

In fact, hypersonic "air-breathing" engines may be the only solution for dramatic reductions in the cost of launching payloads to orbit.

During a recent visit to Australia, I had a chance to visit several defence installations, including a hypersonics research area. I visited with Dr. Allan Paull and members of the Defence Science and Technology Organization (DSTO) hypersonic team located close to Brisbane, Australia.

Dr. Paull made it clear that the team was small but effective.

"We combine the skills of several disciplines, but each member of the team takes ownership of the entire effort and provides inputs to each and every aspect of the enterprise.

"We are not organized around a model of deep pocket experts who stay within the confines of their specialty; we interact across the enterprise to push the research effort forward."

Dr. Paull emphasized that the hypersonic effort required progress in several technologies at the same time, materials, propulsion, computation, etc.

The Aussies are building a number of hypersonic vehicles and doing ground tests on these vehicles and preparing for future flight tests as well. Tests for the HIFiRE program are performed on an extraordinary test range, the Woomera Test Range, in South Australia. This is a very large area where the vehicles can be recovered and then fully examined to determine their performance parameters. It is not a well-instrumented range, but with proper funding, could be.

The US hypersonics program needs a practical focus, as well as a funding and priority boost.

Partnering with Australia can boost the effort by providing for a best value partner, an effective test range, innovative thinking, and capabilities from that partner, and an ability to provide that partner with capabilities which they themselves may either lack or would find prohibitively expensive to provide.

For example, if one wished to do a test replicating what the Chinese just did, it would cost three to five times more in the United States than in Australia. By building a solid working relationship and joint development, access to the Australian range would make sense for both sides and a more cost effective and capable result in a timely manner could be achieved.

After my visit, I had a chance to discuss my findings with Dr. Mark Lewis, the former chief scientist of the USAF and a leading researcher in Hypersonics. Dr. Lewis underscored the importance of boosting the partnership going forward for a number of reasons.

"This is an important relationship because the Australians bring significant intellectual contributions to the table. They also have important practical flight experience; we can even argue that they flew the very first flying scramjet under their HyShot program, which was a precursor to HiFIRE. They have an extraordinary test range as well.

"Much like the global F-35 would not exist without allies and partners, the effort to work with core partners on other twenty-first-century

                    ROBBIN F. LAIRD

capabilities is crucial as well. There is none so more than a steadily and fully funded Australian-U.S. partnership in hypersonics.[5]

5.

https://sldinfo.com/2014/05/australia-works-hypersonics-for-21st-century-capabilities-a-key-american-partner-for-pacific-defence/

Chapter Five

Australia and the Global Competiton

Australia has for most of its history been a junior partner to a global partner. First it was part of the British empire, and then part of the American empire which emerged from World War II. Both empires are now part of history.

Both countries remain key allies for Australia as the AUKUS launch would suggest. The problem is that AUKUS was an initiative of three politically troubled leaders and just how this trilateral defence cooperation will really work out is an open question.

Australia as a remote continent, could work with its senior partners as part of that partners' broader global strategy without really worrying about direct attacks on Australian soil. That of course changed with the Japanese strike on Darwin and in the battle of the Coral Sea.

It has only been in the current era as Communist China became a global economic power with growing military capabilities to project globally that once again Australia had to consider the threat directly to Australia.

The Perspective of Dibb and Brabin-Smith

In a paper written by Paul Dibb and Richard Brabin-Smith and published in 2021, the changed nature of the threat to Australia was highlighted in terms of the loss of the buffer zone provided by geography. As the authors warn: "Australia now needs to implement serious changes to how warning time is considered in defence planning. The need to plan for reduced warning time has implications for the Australian intelligence community, defence strategic policy, force structure priorities, readiness, and sustainability. Important changes will also be needed with respect to personnel, stockpiles of missiles and munitions, and fuel supplies.

"We can no longer assume that Australia will have time gradually to adjust military capability and preparedness in response to emerging threats. In other words, there must be a new approach in defence to managing warning, capability, and preparedness, and detailed planning for rapid expansion and sustainment."

The United States remains the key ally in addressing the Chinese military threat for many reasons, but the United States will be preoccupied in crises impacting its own interests as well. This means that an expanded focus on building out Australian buffer capabilities will be significant to shaping an effective response to reduced warning times.

New digital technologies have altered the question of what warning time is all about. Notably, with regard to the cyber threats, when is there an attack, and what does it mean? As the authors note: "A campaign of cyberattack and intensified cyber-exploitation against Australia could be launched with little notice, given the right level of motivation, and would have the advantage of having at least a level of plausible deniability while imposing limits to what might be envisaged as a proportional response. Such response options available to Australia would include retaliation, such as a government-sanctioned cyberattack—a capability that the Australian Government has acknowledged it has. (This capability has already been used against terrorists, but whether it has been used more widely isn't publicly known.)

"The warning time for the need to conduct such operations is potentially very short, meaning that there needs to be a high level of preparedness, including the ability quickly to expand the cyber workforce (with a concomitant need for expedited security clearances), and cyberattack campaigns that are thought out well in advance. There's a strong argument that such planning should include within its scope the possibility of causing high levels of damage to the adversary's infrastructure."[1]

Inherent in their argument are several key considerations facing Australia in terms of allies and adversaries. First, with a direct threat to Australia itself, how will Australia shape capabilities to defend itself, notably when the range of attack mechanisms has expanded with the digital age? What is the relationship between how Australia might do so and the interests and capabilities of its allies, the United States and Japan, being the most significant? How will the Chinese adversary shape a campaign plan against Australia within the broader context of a Pacific attack and defence strategy?

How will Australia find ways to harmonise whatever direct defence capabilities it shapes with those of its core allies? How will such efforts

---

1. https://www.aspi.org.au/report/deterrence-through-denial-strat egy-era-reduced-warning-time

be viewed by Pacific nations who are at best partners, or at worst de facto window watchers or allies of the Chinese? How will Australia find ways to be able to talk directly with Chinese leaders and shape responses which would be in the Australian interest?

These challenges are in turn deepened by the dramatic changes underway within the societies of both the United Kingdom and the United States. And those changes clearly require shaping engagement strategies by Australia to influence perceptions and policies within those nations of what Australia will and will not do in terms of regional and global defence.

Or put another way, with a withdrawal from being a part of a greater empire, Australia will focus on policies and capabilities which it considers crucial for its own defence, working closely with the militaries of its allies, notably the United States and Japan, but well aware that when push comes to shove, the allies might well have different interests and different solutions to manage a crisis.

The Perspective of Brendan-Sargeant

This then leads to a major challenge not only facing Australia but notably for Australia, namely thinking through how to work more effectively with allies, partners, and adversaries to steer outcomes it can support and arguably in their interest. In the late Brendan Sargeant's view, such a shift is a major one for Australia. And in my discussions with him shortly before he died, we discussed why this was so. Over the years, I had many discussion with Brendan starting with his time in Washington when I was working with Secretary Wynne.

Sargeant underscored in my last interview with him that a country's identity is closely tied up with what its strategic assumptions are and how those assumptions craft a narrative. "A country is an imagined community—it possesses an identity created by the people who live within it, the stories these people embody and tell, both as individuals and communities. A country is a larger and more complex entity than any individual human being, but as an imagined community, a country does not exist without the people who have created it out of their actions, stories, desires, and their sense of who they are and where they belong.

"A country will possess a strategic imagination which will have evolved over time in response to the influence of geography, history, culture, and the many other tangible and intangible forces that go to create a community and its vision of itself. A country's strategic imagination is a living thing, dynamic and evolving in contact with the world, and full of contradictions. In those rare moments in a country's history where a genuine choice must be made and action taken, a country's strategic imagination becomes most visible."

This is notably important for Australia as it faces a major shift in its strategic focus from building defence capabilities for engagement in what has been labelled "the global commons" in support of a "rules-based order" to defending Australia itself against adversaries who fully intend to shape a global order serving their interests, not what remains of a liberal democratic order.

This is how Sargeant put it in that last interview: "Perhaps the deep purpose of strategic policy is to help create Australia by charting a future and giving meaning to the past. Strategic policy and its expression in action through strategy builds national identity; national identity validates strategy. Yet our language can lack authenticity. We use terms such as 'creative middle power' to describe ourselves—or we 'punch above our weight.'

"These are clichés, a tired rhetoric designed to mobilize political support and unlock resources, provide talking points for politicians and officials. Our policy and strategic documents repeatedly reference the 'rules-based global order' and of the U.S. Alliance as the foundation of our security. We avoid the arduous task of self-creation and instead deploy these clichés as a shield against our anxieties. Yet the Indo-Pacific asks us: how long will this rhetoric, increasingly nostalgic in tone, make sense?"

The question of where Australia fits into the evolving Indo-Pacific world, and how to shape a realistic and effective leadership role, is a key one for the liberal democracies. With the twenty-first-century authoritarian states clearly focused on making the world a thriving place for their culture, their economies, and their way of life, they have worked inside the systems of the liberal democracies through various means as well as directly assaulted them globally.

And as the global authoritarian powers shape global reach, how does this change the situation for Australia? Sargeant addressed this in part in his discussion of strategic space. "Australian strategic policy and strategy have always grappled with the profound influence of geography as both a constraint and an opportunity. Australia's geography provides challenges in communications, logistics, and force disposition.

"From a strategic perspective, it provides both the luxury and the challenge of distance. In a strategic environment of reducing strategic space, the challenge for Australian strategy is to determine which force disposition and design is going to provide the most flexibility and embody the best recognition of the reality of our strategic environment.

"In this context, how we conceptualize our strategic geography in the context of a changing strategic order is a challenge to strategic imagination at many levels and in many ways. We live in a maritime environment, but on a continent-sized island. Australia has a history of sending expeditionary forces to other parts of the world as part of a larger alliance or coalition engagement on the basis that Australian security is often best served by participation and maintenance of larger global strategic systems from which Australia benefits.

"Yet Australia is also an island continent, which brings with it a concomitant obligation to provide for its defence, but also creates a sense of security because any invading adversary would face almost insurmountable obstacles.

"But is this changing? We have always thought about geography as providing us with space. But in a world where space as a strategic resource is diminishing, do we need to reconceptualize our strategic geography to take us beyond, for example, the demarcation of continent versus archipelago, or do we need to see that geographical space as a single continuous environment? In this context, recent developments in Australian strategic environment have emphasized the need to focus on our near region as an arena for strategic contestation.

"This has given a renewed prominence to the question of our strategic geography, our capacity for self-reliance and the terms of our participation in larger regional and global strategic systems. How we understand and conceptualize our geography is an imaginative challenge before it becomes a challenge for policy and strategy."

The Challenge Posed by the Uncertain Future of the United Kingdom

With the death of Queen Elizabeth II, the world was reminded that Australia is part of the British Commonwealth. But with the ascension of Charles III, the Commonwealth itself will shrink. And the United Kingdom itself is under significant pressures to remain that.

The decision to withdraw from the European Union followed by the global impact of the pandemic on the United Kingdom which has slowed the process of working a post-European relationship for the United Kingdom, raises fundamental questions about Britain's place in the world. In place of its earlier empire, what Britain has on offer is what its leaders have called "global Britain." But the problem is that Britain is no longer a global power. And its significant economic crisis shared by many Western states will limit its ability to shape a world in its own making.

In many ways, Britain is on a survival course reminiscent of the challenges facing it when Mrs. Thatcher became the prime minister. And with the Brexit withdrawal and with a very modest military, the question of how the United Kingdom will sort through its future defence posture, capabilities, and priorities is a significant one.

In spite of the effort of former Prime Minister Boris Johnson during his time in power to visibly support Ukraine and to donate weapons to that state, the priority for Britain will be Northern Europe, the North Sea, and the Greenland–Iceland UK gap in the North Atlantic. Similar to the Australian re-prioritisation, the return of geography is very likely to shape Britain's approach to defence in ways that will limit its ability to contribute in any meaningful way to the direct defence of Australia and the Indo-Pacific region.

During a 2019 visit to London, a senior defence official flat out stated to me: "With the return of geography, the focus needs to be clearly on our Northern and Southern Flanks, and this means the emphasis needs to be placed upon air–naval integration. The Royal Navy and the RAF need to find ways to work much more effective integration. And our new carrier provides a means whereby we can do so."

With Brexit Britain, there is a natural withdrawal of military attention from what used to be called the Central Front during the Cold War days, and a renewed focus is on the flanks. France and Germany have asserted that their defence collaboration will take care of Europe's defence and provide the manoeuvre forces and space for the defence of Europe's new frontline in Poland and the Baltics, and the United Kingdom's contribution will be reduced to reinforcing efforts, not leading them in this continental European sector.

In a way, this is a similar trajectory for Australia but in its case, the strategic space is the first island chain for Australia back to the continent. In other words, strategic threats and priorities are reinforcing regional geo-political interests and prioritisation on those interests for the nations and their defence establishments.

The significant financial challenges facing Britain certainly put into question the reality of any real growth in defence, and the ongoing political crises puts into question the ability of the government to direct a "united" kingdom. This means that the services will be looking to achieve what they can from leveraging the current platforms but finding ways for greater integration as a joint and coalition force. And clearly, such an effort is similar to Australia and co-learning will take place.

A good evaluation of the reality facing UK forces was provided by Chris Morris in a January 2022 article. Here he argued that UK planning had become very unrealistic with regard to the force modernisation which really would occur and the impact of having reduced military in terms of force capabilities, as its largest ally—the United States—faced similar challenges. "Ultimately, were the United Kingdom to envision a more hostile and threatening future, this would reveal the negative repercussions of failing to invest in more established warfighting domains. Facing up this future might initially force the

United Kingdom to confront its declining capacity. But this experience need not be entirely negative. The United Kingdom will certainly struggle to maintain a reasonably sized conventional military, and even if it invests in the cyber and space domains, it is unlikely to match the spending of both adversaries and allies alike. Acknowledging the true scale of the challenge could lead the United Kingdom to seek out more creative routes forward. Rather than replicating the course that other, more capable nations are taking on a smaller scale, engaging with the limitations that the United Kingdom is facing could spur the nation to find new options for offsetting its weaknesses.

"There are, of course, no ideal solutions when faced with a problem of this nature, but acknowledging it is a crucial first step. One route might see the United Kingdom take a more reactive approach, orientating its limited resources around its adversaries' weaknesses as they emerge. Another controversial solution could be to specialize in a single domain of warfighting, rather than try and keep up across the entire spectrum of both established and emergent domains. Whatever path the United Kingdom chooses, accepting the uncomfortable truth about its limited capabilities will be far more productive in the long run."[2]

The community of interest between Britain and Australia remains significant and strong. Both nations are operating similar equipment and their forces work closely together. The AUKUS arrangement is really about expanding the possibilities of working common technological projects to enable more cost-effective force structure development.

---

2. https://warontherocks.com/2022/01/how-the-united-kingdo m-can-confront-its-limited-capabilities/

But a community of interest, even a privileged one is not the same as a strategic compact where engagement in common strategic goals is assumed. Rather strategic goals will differ and priorities diverge in many cases. This is the nature of the alliance structure facing the United Kingdom and Australia, one in which specifics will need to be worked out rather than delivered by some "hidden hand" of global cooperation.

Britain and Australia could well see enhanced sharing of defence manpower as Australia faces very significant skills shortages. And given the "special relationship" between the two, the transfer of retired personnel from Britain to Australia could be important in selected areas of defence development in Australia itself.

Britain leaving the European Union means for Australia that the UK is no longer a way into continental Europe and its technology and resources. It is now incumbent on Australia to work specific relationships with key European allies and with the European Union (EU). And these considerations will rival any "special relationship" with Britain itself.

It is notable that when the EU was working a new trade relationship with China in 2020, that Australia and Japan worked closely together to lobby the EU to not go ahead with the project as designed, and the two countries working together did affect the EU policy.

In my January 2021 interview with Ross Babbage, the noted strategist highlighted the challenge. "The proposed agreement sends the wrong messages and I think it's a very poor move. In particular, it displays no sort of solidarity with the democracies in Asia and the broader Indo-Pacific. "It's not only Australia that has been pressured by Beijing. Look at what the Chinese regime has been doing to the Indians, the Vietnamese, the Indonesians, the Malaysians, the Filipinos, and also the Japanese, the South Koreans, and the Taiwanese. There is also the Chinese regime's behavior in the island states of the South Pacific.

"Some influential Europeans seem not to regard this track record as being terribly important in their calculations. Look at how the Xi regime has performed in keeping its obligations under the WTO, and also their obligations under the free trade agreements they have with Australia and other countries. What faith can Europeans have that the regime in Beijing will abide by any of the agreement's terms?

"There is also the question of helping President Xi out when he is under political and economic pressure at home. The Chinese regime pushed hard for this agreement so as to demonstrate to its own public that it was making good progress internationally. Does Europe really want to give this authoritarian regime such a break?

"In addition, the regime has been eager to conclude the European agreement to give some diplomatic maneuver space, vis-à-vis Washington. They wanted to be seen to be not beholden entirely to the new U.S. administration, no matter what direction it takes. I think they have been very keen to get an agreement with someone to give them extra leverage in Washington. And if that someone was the EU, terrific."

The need to work continental Europe—not following the UK or U.S. lead—is now part of the challenges facing the Australian alliance policies.

And the growing salience of the requirement to have secure supply chains means as well that targeted working relationships in specific areas of supply need to be identified and worked. And this will not happen with broad general G-7 agreements. Rather working specific agreements with various producers globally to deny Chinese dominance and to ensure Australian interests are crucial, such as working a lithium supply chain agreements or similar specific rare earth minerals.

The driver here needs to be a whole of government and society effort to identify key supplies or resources which Australia needs or has and to work specific arrangements with allies and partners, regionally and globally. Such a task could not succeed simply by relying on a special relationship with any one state. There is no automaticity in such an effort; rather it will require clearly targeted analytical efforts and policy priorities worked regionally and globally, sometimes with close allies and in other cases with partners of various political persuasions.

The Challenge Posed by the Uncertain Future of the United States

Alliances are changing and with it the challenge facing Australia to work new approaches and methods to protect its interests and to provide for its direct defence. Nowhere is that truer than working with its most significant military partner, the United States.

The ADF buys and operates a very significant amount of American kit and does so for a very simple reason—it is the best available in the liberal democratic world. It is also the case that the working relationships between the U.S. and Australian militaries is really first rate. The forces like to work together, and there is a very high level of trust between them.

As Paul Dibb put it: "It has become fashionable recently to call for Australia to consider how we might navigate a new world alone without America. My colleague, Hugh White, has gone as far as proclaiming that Australia's dependence on the US has been largely abandoned and, instead, Australia is seeking its security principally as part of a coalition of Asian countries—or what he calls call 'an Asian NATO'—to contain China.

"These claims are not supported by a close reading of the recently released 2020 Defence Strategic Update in which the Prime Minister and Defence Minister have made it plain that the Government 'will continue to deepen our alliance with United States.' The Update emphasises that the security arrangements, interoperability, intelligence sharing, and technological and industrial cooperation between Australia and the United States 'are critical to Australia's national security.'

"The most important example of the increasingly close relationship we are planning to have with the U.S. is the fact that Australia is going to spend in excess of $100 billion on missiles and strike weapons to increase the ADF's maritime deterrence and long-range land strike capabilities. These missiles include maritime guided weapons, deployed ballistic and high-speed missiles, high-speed, long-range strike capability, as well as air-launched strike missiles. And just from where—other than the US—do the 'let's abandon the US alliance' types think we are going to acquire such sophisticated missiles?

"Another example of our increased reliance on the U.S. is the fact that without access to highly classified US defence technology, the ADF would not be a credible force capable of fighting high-intensity conflict against emerging regional systems. Australia has the most capable fifth-generation air force in our region, but our Joint Strike Fighters and Growler EW Super Hornets depend crucially on huge amounts of highly classified operational mission data from the U.S. In effect, this means we are integrated into the U.S. military system."[3]

All of this can be true, but at the same, the nature of alliances associated with the United States and thereby that of Australia with the United States is changing as well. The proclamation of a new AUKUS

---

3. https://defence.info/dannys-corner/2020/11/implications-of-the-u-s-elections-for-australias-defence-policy/

alliance in 2021 was made by three politically challenged leaders and really is about the submarine issues, including deployments and acquisition in the coming years of a new capability to be based and built in Australia.

But in reality, it is not a new alliance, and in the case of President Biden, the announcement provided an opportunity to gain some press when he had just orchestrated a blitzkrieg withdrawal from Afghanistan. The Blitzkrieg withdrawal delivered a key blow to the American defence approach of the past twenty years. The United States prioritised and built a force designed for land wars and atrophied its global power projection forces.

In his book *Danger on our Doorstep* by the late Senator Jim Molan, the author highlighted the significant hiatus created by the American prioritisation on the land wars.

"The U.S. is surfacing from decades of war in the Middle East with worn-out equipment, understandably having allocated a lot of its funding to 'today's wars' rather than investing in the future. During the Iraq War, for instance, Secretary of Defence Bob Gates wanted more drones to carry on the day-to-day fight in Iraq and found himself in conflict with the U.S. Air Force, which wanted to continue building the fighters and bombers that it thought would be needed in the future.

"Gates sacked the chief of the US Air Force and restricted the production of aircraft such as the stealth F-22 fighter and the B-21 bomber, in order to build the drones and other aircraft he needed. The result was that only a limited number of the extraordinary F-22s were built and the B-21 is still not in production. The impact of diverted spending and focus will be felt for a long time to come. The likely war with China, if it is ever fought by weapons of this type, is going to be fought by a very small number of modern stealth fighters, but mainly by U.S. fighters and bombers that are 20 to 30 years old."[4]

When I worked for the Secretary of the USAF, Michael Wynne, I experienced first-hand this very significant strategic shift. Rather than prioritising the Navy and the Air Force, which makes the most sense for the United States given its geography, the U.S. Army led the way. What joint warfighting developed in those twenty years was support by the navy and the air force to the army, not the kind of joint warfighting we need against the Chinese, to take a case in point.

How rapidly can the United States rebuild the relevant military force necessary for global power projection? And will the U.S. Army's dominance of the American strategy end any time soon?

In addition, there is little question that there is a significant impact of the Afghan Blitzkrieg Withdrawal Strategy on the U.S. military as it engages in a strategic shift from the land wars to a focus on great power competition. Nearly a million Americans served in Afghanistan along with thousands of allied soldiers and officers. Because this was a lengthy engagement, characterised as stability operations and nation building, those soldiers and officers trained and worked with Afghans closely to shape a way ahead, because that is the very heart of managed transition. Then suddenly those relationships are cut by the U.S. leadership, leaving those soldiers and officers in the position of having to confront the loss, death, torture, or relocation of those very persons with whom they worked for a "new" Afghanistan.

The Obama Administration promised a Pacific pivot, which largely did not happen because of the demands from CENTCOM and the Middle East, including the rise of ISIS and the Syrian civil war. In

---

4. Jim Molan, Danger on Our Doorstep, HarperCollins. Kindle Edition, p. 106.

fact, it might be remembered that President Biden was Vice President Biden during the period of fighting the "good war" in Afghanistan. The military focus was on counterinsurgency, nation building, and that most ambiguous of terms, stability operations. Shifting from this skill set to preparing for full spectrum crisis management and the high-end fight is significant. How will this happen? Will the United States shape a new counterterrorism strategy in the Middle East which significantly reduces demand on U.S. forces? If not, then frankly, the demand side is beyond what the U.S. military can provide for a strategic shift.

Given that the major threat is the global conflict between authoritarian and liberal democratic powers, the role of the United States is not only reduced but the threats to the liberal democracies are enhanced as well. According to the noted American strategist, Professor Paul Bracken: "What we are seeing is an acceleration of polycentric nationalism. Everybody's relating to everybody else, nervously of trying to keep the balance, and very reluctant to join rigid blocks a la the Cold War because they want to preserve their independence. This situation leads to significant distrust of alliances and enhances the desire to want to have something they can fall back on in the very worst case . . ."[5]

As those U.S. allies who are serious about their own direct defence build out approaches to do so, working with the United States remains significant. The global F-35 force is a key example both in Europe and the Pacific. But at the same time, what can be done practically with the defence force in being? And how best to do so when the America of the times of the arsenal of democracy are clearly no more?

---

5. https://defense.info/re-thinking-strategy/2021/08/the-impact
   -of-the-biden-afghan-withdrawal-on-global-dynamics-the-persp
   ective-of-paul-bracken/

AUKUS can be seen as a call for indeed broadening how an arsenal of democracy can be built going forward. The war in Ukraine has demonstrated how shallow the defence inventories of both Europe and the United States are, and a clear need to focus on defence mobilisation.

Can the United States rebuild its power projection military in a world where the twenty-first-century authoritarian powers have significant global reach? And as it does so, can a national strategy be formed which more realistically captures the real situation of the United States rather than a nostalgic view of itself as a global power it once was in the 1950s?

And to build such a strategy, one would have to overcome the deepening cleavages in the overall fundamental values and priorities of the United States. The states in the United States themselves are deeply divided on approaches to economic development with the national government under Biden prioritising tax, spend, and attack politics on the opposition. It is hardly a unity government. And several Republican states are pursuing very different tax and spend policies and are themselves the leading centres of economic growth in the United States.

In other words, for Australia, the United States remains its key military force ally and partner. But at the same time, the United States has a very uncertain global presence and strategy, increasingly hostage to domestic conflict and politics. This means that there is no plug and play strategy for Australia in terms of its region; but it requires shaping ways ahead of working with the U.S. military and shaping a policy of influence in the United States, as much with specific states as with Washington itself.

Rather than being a capability plugging into an American-led Pacific strategy, Australia must itself shape that strategy with allies and partners in the region, and thereby broadening its own influence to shape what it perceives would be a proper American strategy in the region. But if Australia cannot provide for its direct defence and cannot expand the concrete working relationships with allies and partners in the region, it will not be able to do so.

The Challenge Posed by Co-opetition with the Twenty-First-Century Authoritarian Powers

It has always been challenging for liberal democratic leaders and publics to understand how authoritarian leaders are going to act globally. Currently, we face a very significant global conflict between a coalition of twenty-first-century authoritarian powers and Western-style democracies, and regional powers in various parts of the world that are not part of either world.

What we have seen in the context of the conflict in Ukraine is authoritarian powers providing through an arsenal of authoritarian's weapons and economic support to Russia. Western states have also provided aid through a competing arsenal of democracy but in fact what has emerged is a clear element of the conflict between both approaches.

The challenge which the democracies need to face is not only one of ensuring as much confluence of interest among themselves but a diversified group of authoritarian states whose common interest is to make the world safe for authoritarians. It really is less about alliances contesting each other than communities of interest forming up in a contested economic and military global battlespace.

China's Belt and Road initiative and its engagement in both Africa and Latin America follow the model of shaping a global informal empire. The Chinese have shaped a global informal empire that is part of their global reach. And that global informal empire provides reach into Latin America and Africa in ways that the West is simply not interested in pursuing collectively.

By trade and investment, China has become a key player in Africa and Latin America. Its practices in doing so have a number of questionable dimensions, but instead of highlighting the reality of Chinese informal empire practices, Western states have largely ignored the opportunity to do so. They have focused on issues like Taiwan and the South China Sea, both very important but not part of the informal empire geopolitical strategy. But the reality is that China poses a global threat to the Western order underwritten by its economic, cultural, and third-world narrative efforts along with an expanding fleet of both military and commercial shipping and ports as well.

For the Chinese with their global economic presence and their focused efforts to leverage globalisation to their strategic advantage, direct investment in strategic industry and transportation infrastructure in Europe has been a clear focus of attention. As Ross Babbage put it in his report on political warfare: "China's very large economy and the authority of the Party within it gives Beijing extensive scope to persuade, bribe, and coerce national and regional governments to accept large infrastructure developments and other Chinese involvements within their societies. China Inc. can afford to purchase key foreign enterprises, offer funding for un-economic infrastructure projects, and heavily subsidize the entry of Chinese corporations into strategically important markets, even within strong Western societies.

This provides Beijing with strategic positioning options that Moscow cannot afford and is not well structured to undertake."[6]

Dealing with the twenty-first-century authoritarians is then not just a military challenge but an economic and cultural one as well. The challenge is to find ways to shape crisis management and combat capabilities to deal with the authoritarians across the spectrum of warfare. It is also a cultural challenge or informational warfare challenge. The Chinese notably have significant influence in virtually all leading global states. They have done this through investments in universities and buying out firms in a number of democratic states. Dealing with this challenge is not simply military but it is cultural.

How does Australia along with its partners continue to work with China or Russia or Iran and at the same time understand how to compete with them? Co-opetition is a term used in business literature about the need to cooperate while competing to achieve market leadership. "In most of the modern theories of business, competition is seen as one of the key forces that keep firms lean and drive innovation," Adam Brandenburger of the Harvard Business School and Barry Nalebuff of the Yale School of Management have challenged that emphasis. They suggest that businesses can gain advantage by means of a judicious mixture of competition and cooperation. Cooperation with suppliers, customers and firms producing complementary or related products can lead to expansion of the market and the formation of new business relationships, perhaps even the creation of new forms of enterprise."

Put in other terms, clearly a state like Australia needs to work with a major power like China, but at the same time, prepare to persuade

---

6. https://defense.info/global-dynamics/2020/12/china-lodges-a
-war-against-australian-sovereignty/

China that it is not worth the risk of war to ramp up coercive strategies against Australia. How can this be done?

In a discussion with Nordic leaders during a visit in 2020, the parameters of how to meet this challenge was highlighted in an interview with the CEO of Risk Intelligence, a Copenhagen-based firm, Hans Tino Hansen discussed the question of the way ahead with regard to European crisis management.

"Even with regard to defence stocks, Denmark, like many nations, has acted on the assumption that when a crisis comes, we can get access to the supplies we want through the free market and just in time. The problem is that when a crisis comes, one of the first thing that happens is a significant disruption of supply chains, and nations will focus on providing for their own needs, and not worrying primarily about their role in the global marketplace. We have certainly seen that with the COVID-19 crisis."

We then discussed the question of how European nations, notably the smaller ones, are going to be able to address supply chain security with crisis management in mind. He argued that "clearly part of the answer is to stockpile what are predictable needs. Finland has never deviated from such a strategy; Sweden and Denmark in the Cold War had a policy similar to Finland; but we have abandoned the Cold War stockpiles, and we have seen the result.

"But the broader problem is that with regard to the wide variety of crises which could occur, you do not always know where the supply chain weakness can be found. You don't know which country will close down its production. You don't know who is going to close down his production lines. You don't know where shipping cannot operate anymore.

"There are a lot of things in play here which makes things a lot more complicated than many people would have thought before

COVID-19. And if we compare this to what would happen in times of armed conflict or a major international crisis, then a similar set of challenges would play out.

"Another part of the answer is to develop and test alternative production capacity including 3D printing options and changing existing high- and low-tech production lines. However, while alternative production lines may be able to assist with certain military and medical equipment for the two scenarios above, it will not be able to produce SM-2 missiles for navy frigates or CT scanners for the hospitals."

We then discussed what he considered a realistic path ahead with regard to better crisis management planning and relevant policy actions in the future. Clearly, a key requirement is to focus realistically on the challenge, both nationally and with core partners.

"We need to address how to think through where the supply chain breaks are likely to happen and with what effects and to shape alternative paths to meet needs in a crisis. Focusing on such planning as a core government requirement along with core allies or trusted partners needs to come back out of the Cold so to speak or literally bring back some of the best aspects of Cold War thinking.

"We also need to abandon the notion that we may be able to get our supplies in a global market at any time. We need to shape collaborative structures as we used to have in NATO in the Cold War period where muscle memory had been shaped and we had a planning approach to leverage."

This is a national approach focused on working specific arrangements with specific partners and understanding that meeting the challenge of dealing with the diverse coalition of authoritarian states will NOT be solved by a single state or automatically from an historically formed alliance.

This is the other side of reworking how to do alliance strategies. Much like reworking how Australia navigates change among its democratic partners, those partners will themselves work out their own ways ahead with the diverse coalition of authoritarian powers. How much convergence or divergence is possible among those democratic partners of Australia? How does Australia forge a national strategy and work specific ways ahead with those partners willing to do so?

In earlier days, for Australia, it was easier to follow the lead of the senior state, whether in the British or American empires. With a global order not assumed but contested, and with clear engagement in the values of the liberal democratic world, how does Australia conduct its relationship with authoritarian powers who have no inclination to support the "rules-based order"?

Shaping an Alliance Strategy in the New Strategic Situation

Australia is headed into new territory when it comes to shaping its alliance working relationships in dealing with its most dangerous regional competitor since Imperial Japan. How to do so and to ensure that Australia is in a realistic position to protect its ability to defend itself and its interests? With China, the challenge is a profound one for a liberal democracy. How to cooperate with a power dedicated to changing the regional and global order to your disadvantage?

Any answer to these questions must start with re-setting the manufacturing agenda of Australia and reworking its commodity relationships with the dominant economic power in the region. What will Australia manufacture, and what will it do in re-shifting its commodities cooperation with desired allies vice China?

A second key consideration is what military strategy makes sense for Australia in the Indo-Pacific and how to influence key allies to engage in the desired strategy. The United States has many strategies in the Indo-Pacific, dependent on military service and what administration is in power and what macro-economic strategy is being pursued by the dominant economy in the liberal democratic world.

To provide for its direct defence, Australia will have to make full use of its territory. This means undoubtedly that its key allies will participate more fully in the use of facilities on Australian soil. Does this mean then that Australia's primary defence effort is to protect the sanctuary with an ability to project power? How far? And for what purpose? If American forces fought forward towards Chinese territory, would Australian forces join them directly or complement them in replacing assets moved forward and operate in their stead in the mid-Pacific?

How would training with the allies—the United States, Japan, and South Korea—be used to shape approaches that make sense to the ADF in support of an Australian Indo-Pacific strategy? Training and exercises can be used to shape strategic approaches.

And more broadly, Australia and the liberal democracies face a major challenge in building a twenty-first-century arsenal of democracy. The United States has put itself in the position whereby it innovates too slowly and builds too expensively to be the arsenal of democracy it was during World War II. Europe has largely ignored defence production as something worthy of an advanced civilisation, although the war in Ukraine might change that.

How can Australia leverage its unique relationship with the allies to generate change as they work to reshape development and production capabilities? It is not simply a question of borrowing the good lessons learned by its allies; it is important for Australia to learn some of those lessons and impart them to allies to become more capable to produce the products collectively needed.

Chapter Six

The Changing Nature of the Chinese Challenge

The Party Congress in Communist China held in March 2023 has both consolidated Xi's control of the Chinese system and turned the country further from its earlier legacy of global engagement built on its powerful export engine. According to my colleague, Dr. Harald Malmgren, Chinese policy under Xi has taken a significant strategic turn in its economy and with it in terms of how he seeks to shape the China of the next decade. This shift has significant implications for a world which is in flux. In this new world order, relationships by multiple power centres which would not be described either as Western or as great power authoritarians have emerged and are shaping new global linkages. And China under Xi is focused on enhancing these relationships at the expense of its recent decades of reliance for high growth on its export relationships with the West.

The Next Phase of the Xi Era

Dr. Harald Malmgren and his colleague Nicholas Glinsman have highlighted and summarised the Chinese shift in their seminal paper written earlier this year, entitled, "China and its Lost Decades Ahead." In this paper, the authors assess that China is moving on from its neo-mercantilist economic model which relied heavily on exports for growth. At the Party Congress, the importance of global exports was replaced by placing highest national priority on domestic consumption within China itself.

The dramatic shift in priority from its external relations in economic growth and the drawdown of their ability to rely on foreign capital to domestic growth drivers poses huge challenges for China in shaping a new way ahead. Malmgren has also noted in a recent discussion I had with him that up till now, President Xi had kept reporting of his military exclusively to himself. All other matters, including state security, were under the direction of the Chinese Communist Party. In March, Xi declared that state security was removed from CCP jurisdiction and would henceforth report exclusively to Xi personally. All matters that he deemed to be essential in managing internal security would be subject to his personal decisions. Thus, from now on, the entire CCP was subordinated to the supreme leader, and the Party would function under decisions made by state security and the Central Military Commission, which Xi chairs.

To better control the domestic economy, Xi has decided to intensify centralised direction of all segments of the economy. Since Deng, state-owned enterprises had been subject to Party direction, but large segments of the economy functioned with considerable autonomy. Xi made it clear that he wanted greater public and private coordination, and that Party political officials would be placed into the management of all private businesses.

Moreover, the Party would assign its officials to participate in all scientific research projects and the development of technological innovations. This would, of course, complicate relations between Chinese scientific innovators who were participating with American scientists and investors, calling into question whether either the Party or the U.S. Government would permit continuation of such ongoing businesses and R&D projects. Innovations which had been spurred by foreign investments and engagements of various foreign academics and scientists would likely be re-crafted to become more Soviet-like with commissars within the key companies and domestic economic sectors.

The COVID-19 Pandemic lockdowns paralysed the Chinese economy during the period from the start of 2020 to the very end of 2022. Throughout the world markets, there has been an expectation that the end of the 2023 pandemic would result in a strong Chinese economy rebound, bringing back to life the powerful Chinese engine of growth that had long provided momentum to the rest of the world. As it turned out, 2023 showed little signs of a Chinese rebound. New orders for exports did not appear. Demand for ocean-going cargo carriers remained depressed.

What the world had forgotten was that world trade in manufactures had already slowed down in the years since the Great Financial Crisis of 2008–09. During 2019, just before the pandemic struck, the IMF warned that a synchronised industrial downturn was evident throughout the world. The pandemic then took over, slowing and even halting all economic activity virtually everywhere. Now, in post-pandemic world of 2023, much of the world is back where the economy of 2019 left off—in an economic downturn.

None of the world's great trading nations, Japan, China, South Korea, Germany, or the United States, showed any signs of increased demand for manufactures, whether automobiles or consumer appliances. Worldwide inflation was being attacked by central banks everywhere, raising interest rates to subdue spending and rising wage demands.

In February 2023, the Government Investment Corporations of Singapore, one of the world's biggest Sovereign Wealth Funds, announced that it was pulling back from exposure to investments in China. This agency is known throughout the world as the most knowledgeable entity able to make objective assessments of the inner workings of the Chinese economy.

The U.S. Government was also showing concern about U.S. private investment into China that might be supporting technologies of national security concern. This was casting a negative blanket over previous years of optimism among high-tech American and European technology investors.

Malmgren noted that China has reached an economic plateau similar to that reached by Japan in the late 1980s, where Japan shifted its economic growth to direct engagement in the United States and other Western states. China will not be able to do that because of the Western concern with regard to how China has distorted "globalisation" to its advantage.

According to Malmgren, with the United States cutting the umbilical cord to its technology and technological investments, there is growing Chinese recognition that their own pace of innovation could slow significantly.

With the economic slowdown by China, the role which China played in the 2008 global economic crisis will not be repeated. The authors concluded in their paper that "China will not come to the world's rescue, as it did in 2008–09 under Hu Jintao."

Malmgren also underscored that the focus on enhanced domestic consumption will prove difficult as well with the economic drawdown and internal protests. Most of the major protests have been highly disciplined in forms that the government felt unable to contain.

These protests have taken two forms: the so-called white paper protest whereby significant numbers of Chinese have simply hoisted blank paper in protest without actually indicating what they are protesting.

The second is that Chinese parents of child-bearing age are refusing to have children and, wives asserting their rights to continue active professional lives and simply avoiding raising any children. The birth rate per thousand Chinese continues to fall dramatically, alongside a growing number of the elderly. The total number of Chinese counted in 2022 showed year on year decline, and the world population experts are now forecasting a steep decline in Chinese population over the next fifty or hundred years.

I will include here with the first part of their paper, a paper which brings together a wide range of data supporting their arguments.

"In late October, when Xi Jinping consolidated his hold on China's communist party at its five-yearly congress, the world cringed. Xi seemed determined to push China back to the age of Mao Zedong, his role model. Hardline ideology would tighten its grip on the world's second-largest economy, with dire implications for the rest.

"The last thing anyone expected from a strongman president entering his 11th year in power was a sudden about face with regard to his policies. Yet within weeks, Xi's government reversed its efforts to control COVID-19, Big Tech companies, the Chinese property market and more. It has shown signs of reduced support for Russia's war in Ukraine while trying to ease diplomatic tensions with the US and in its territorial disputes regarding the South China Sea. This softening seemed so uncharacteristic of Xi that rumors began circulating that his political power was weakening, as other high officials were intervening to alter policy.

"That's unlikely, given that at the congress, Xi had purged enemies and installed allies throughout the party. Yet the 180-degree turn on multiple policy fronts was unmistakable and raises doubts about everything the world thought it knew about Xi, the unbending hardliner. Was he now bending to pressure from worried officials, the public, the deteriorating economy?

"The answer may be all of the above. Xi's COVID-19 policy, the tech crackdown and the property bust had brought the economy to a standstill in 2022. The economy contracted in the fourth quarter, which is likely to bring growth for the year down to 3 percent. That is according to official Chinese data; the reality was probably worse, as the reliability of such has declined under Xi. Nevertheless, and back on point, China has not grown this slowly since the late 1970s and is growing no faster than the rest of the world, also a first since the 1970s.

"A performance that weak was a serious threat to an authoritarian state that rests its legitimacy on promises to restore China's prosperity and its global stature. As the slowdown fueled street rallies against the pursuit of 'zero-COVID-19 lockdowns,' some protesters dared to call for Xi to step down. Officials in his own government were reportedly urging him to act to save the economy. Still, few if any China watchers thought the paramount leader would change course.

"Aiming to revive the economy after the congress, Xi's government started sounding less Maoist. It has dropped the 'three red lines' on borrowing by developers, and announced that the 'rectification' campaign against fintech firms is nearly complete. After tightening state control for years, it is sending out messages of support to the private sector, even offering details of its new global data market that suggest respect for private data ownership.

"The irony: Xi may be trying impractically hard to revive growth. His plans to build 'a modern socialist economy' imply an annual gross domestic product growth target of 5 percent, which is no longer possible. China's population growth has slowed sharply, as has productivity growth. With fewer workers and slumping output per worker, the country's potential growth rate is 2.5 percent. Beyond this year, when spending by Chinese consumers released from lockdown may temporarily boost growth, 5 percent is an unrealistic target. And more debt-financed spending will only increase China's already massive debt load.

"Global investors, who often blow hot and cold on China, have again flipped, this time to embrace the new Xi. Before November, the country's stock market was tanking with the economy. Foreign fund managers were launching emerging market mandates excluding China. Now, they are bullish on hopes of a post-pandemic 'reopening' bounce and have been pouring money into Chinese stocks. The benchmark MSCI China index is up a staggering 50 percent since the late October lows.

"Yet questions about China's policy direction remain. Xi's pivot is a pragmatic course correction, but it raises doubts about his steadiness. His impulse to control may reassert itself when the economy starts to recover.

"However, we just do not see it lasting, and hence there will be no repeat of the Chinese reaction to the Great Financial Crisis of 2008/09, wherein the enormous stimulus introduced by the Hu Jintao administration was accredited with helping the world economy avoid a broad and deep global recession.

"Back to the present and despite the dangers, there are nevertheless signs that the economy is stirring. Subway ridership in major cities is rapidly returning to normal. Consumers who accumulated savings while shut in their homes for much of the past year have money to spend. And the government is rolling out policies to support a rebound, or more accurately, reversing policies that had previously constrained growth. China's ability to recover from nearly three years of self-imposed isolation 'is very likely the single most important factor for global growth in 2023,' according to Kristalina Georgieva, the managing director of the IMF.

"Indeed, the global economy's other main engines are far from firing on all cylinders. The US economy, despite a strong end to 2022, will struggle this year as higher interest rates bite, according to the World Bank's latest forecast. Europe is in recession, and Japan is projected to eke out just a 1 percent growth rate.

"As for China, the World Bank forecasts growth of 4.4 percent this year, and of course, some private estimates are even higher. Goldman predicts a 5.2 percent gain. 'Evidence of a rapid China reopening is accumulating,' the investment bank said in a note to clients last week.

"Still, it will take time for the Chinese to re-establish their pre-pandemic routines, including links to the outside world that the government severed in hopes of keeping the virus at bay. The next few months may bring a stop-and-go recovery before a more widespread resumption of activity in the spring.

"Even with a smooth Chinese reopening, the global economy faces a year of anaemic growth, according to World Bank and IMF projections. As mentioned above, China could theoretically provide a big world economic impetus, but we do not expect China to have growth surge and ride to the rest of the world's rescue.

"One area that commentators are expecting a growth impetus is Chinese exports, but we would argue against that too . . ."

In other words, we are seeing a sharp break from the economic orientation of China and from how China has engaged with the West economically. How then does this affect China's place in the world, and affect the evolution of the evolving global situation and order?

China's Strategic Shift: What Are the Implications for the Evolving Global Order?

The shift from an export-oriented growth economy which is deeply intertwined with the developments in the Western world to one more focused on domestic consolidation and a global shift to the rest of the non-Western world carries with it significant implications for the global competition with the West.

How can we characterise this shift?

What is the nature of the changed competition?

What are the implications for the West?

Although it is early days in providing answers to these questions, we can identify some possible key developments and questions going forward.

The nature of the new global order will be determined by competition among key states and how they cooperate or don't in shaping what has been called frequently a "rules-based order." There might be several "rules-based orders" rather than one as the outcome.

The kind of authoritarian regime being crafted by President Xi and his allies puts a priority on how to shape working relationships with other authoritarian powers. The relationship with Russia is the most visible for China, but there is a global effort to come to terms with other authoritarian powers built around working relationships shaped by the enemy-of-my-enemy-is-my-friend dynamic.

We are simply not very good at analysing how authoritarian leaders work with one another, how they think, how they act, and how they are deterred from actions we fear or do not like. We need to recognise that this is a key field of study which has little to do with how liberal democracies compete and cooperate with one another.

This raises a key question when we address conflict and notably military conflict in the years ahead. We have coined a series of concepts such as hybrid warfare and grey zone conflict which simply reflect that we don't know how to deter, let alone compete in an area which is neither hard nor soft power nor in which force is used to gain objectives short of a major war. The American-led wars in Iraq and Afghanistan have demonstrated that the art of statecraft in dealing with this level of conflict is in short supply.

Authoritarian leaders clearly do not all think alike and have their own version of their national interest. How do and will they work together? How do and will they influence each other?

For example, when President Xi restored the former Chinese name to Vladivostok, how did Putin discern its meaning?

How in fact can Western states most effectively influence authoritarian behaviour?

The track record with regard to Putin certainly is not a showcase for European or American statecraft. What would have deterred him from the Ukraine invasion?

This is a subject worthy of analysis, not from the minds of Westerners but from the mind of Putin and his allies. This is hardly just historical analysis because it is tied up with how we would end such a war and deal with the evolving global order.

Another key area to explore are the changes in the global economy associated with the projected shift led by President Xi. This can be seen on many levels but here I will focus on two.

The first is the need for foreign capital to fuel Chinese domestic development. The recent peace overture led by China with Saudi Arabia and Iran was largely interpreted as dealing with oil and the future energy needs of China. But it is much broader than that.

The American political process led by Biden attacked the legitimacy of the ruler of Saudi Arabia, and Biden turned his back on the Abraham Accords. President Xi couldn't care less about the internal ethics of the Saudi leader but the global future of Saudi is important. They are building new technologies and new defence systems which China could support. China has personnel to replace the current heavy reliance on Pakistanis and the Saudis have capital to invest.

The second is the shift associated with the West and China. There is a clear shift towards innovation in terms of energy, of better use of resources which are loosely associated with dealing with the global climate change.

In dealing with this new phase or age of innovation, there is a shift towards critical minerals and other commodities of enhanced importance, somewhat reminiscent of the shift from coal to oil at the beginning of the twentieth century.

Countries which have these critical minerals and commodities are in a pole position for enhanced global influence and the reshaping of the "rules-based order" to their advantage.

The visit of President Lula to China can be seen in this light. Brazil is not simply part of the South or the developing world. Brazil should be described differently with the Western world increasingly preoccupied with the "climate emergency."

But such a shift in terms of global economic focus raises the question of how Xi will balance his calculation in terms of the use of force and for what purpose with his shift away from the Western economies.

Does an invasion of Taiwan make any sense from his point of view in terms of the global fallout from his shift away from the West?

Or does it become more desirable as a show of force which can enhance his ability to demonstrate the weakness and "moral bankruptcy" of the West?

Then I would like to raise an issue very relevant to the future direction of military conflict. Dr. Pippa Malmgren, Hal's daughter and a noted global analyst in her own right, has raised for some time the secular change in operational capabilities for military forces associated with the growth of AI-enabled machines.

Recently, she argued the following: "The next war for China is a digital operation run by highly responsive and obedient self-replicating robotics, informed by the best data sets and AI that exists anywhere in the world today. Humans won't even be needed for decision-making. In conjunction with super-computing, AI is replacing Generals, especially as the warzone expands beyond a battlefield and across the entire supply chain."[1]

If we look at the question of what one is prepared to do in terms of machine-led destruction to support your version of statecraft, how will China led by President Xi use his machines to support grey zone operations or his global reach?

---

1. https://defense.info/re-shaping-defense-security/2023/03/war-i n-an-era-of-intelligent-machines-whats-the-war-medal-of-the-di gital-era/

I would like to close with some sobering thoughts. Will the West really rebuild their ability to defend their interests? Will we really find ways to work supply chains in common? Will we be able to recover the art of statecraft along with military force innovations to provide deterrence of the authoritarian powers with China being a key leader? And will the West do so while being able to find ways to cooperate with China in those areas that are critical for global survival?

Accompanying the economic shift described by Harald Malmgren might as well be a broader global shift. China would shift from being the economic export growth engine of globalisation as understood by the West.The focus would be upon managing the economic drawdown internally but working globally with key authoritarian allies and non-Western countries in the South to create an alternative to the legacy of a rules-based order.China does not have to be formally allied to other authoritarian powers but just play off what the challenges these powers pose to the West.

And with the Brazils of the world, new resource and trade relationships can be built as alternatives to the capital-intensive belt and road approach.[2] The growth of China's informal empire becomes a key priority for the Chinese leadership as opposed to the export engine to the West. China has focused under the regime of President Xi on building out its global informal empire. By trade and investment, China has become a key player in Africa and Latin America. Its practices in doing so have a number of questionable dimensions, but instead of highlighting the reality of Chinese informal empire practices, Western states have largely ignored the opportunity to do so. They have focused

---

2. https://defense.info/global-dynamics/2023/04/lula-and-xi-in -the-evolving-new-world-order/

on issues like Taiwan and the South China Sea, both very important but not part of the informal empire geopolitical strategy.

But the reality is that China poses a global threat to the Western order underwritten by its economic, cultural, and third-world narrative efforts along with an expanding fleet of both military and commercial shipping and ports as well.

If one looks at the world from the perspective of the Southern Hemisphere, and with the notion of informal empire in mind, one gets a different understanding of how things might play out. If one looks at a map calibrated from the perspective of the Southern Hemisphere and looks from China outward towards South America and Africa, one begins to see why Australia for example becomes more important in the way ahead for China as a global power and player.

As far as military issues go, China has internal problems—significant and growing. But in terms of defence, their nuclear arms build-up makes them a territory one would not wish to strike, and with the growing domination of Russia, the internal resource trade routes are secure.

This means that their outreach with regard especially to naval power becomes more significant, less in terms of directly confronting the United States and the West, than building a force that can operate globally around them. At the same time, building a global navy of course enhances their ability directly to deter or fight the West if it comes to that. The recent exercises off of South Africa with the Russians illustrate this approach.[3]

---

3. https://www.npr.org/2023/02/18/1158169215/south-africa-joins-russia-and-china-in-naval-exercises

The Key Elements of Deterrence in Dealing with the Chinese Challenge

Ross Babbage in his new book, *The Next Major War: Can the U.S. and its Allies Win Against China?* takes the wider view of the Chinese military challenge.[4] Rather than limiting himself to a force-on-force analysis, he looks at the broader nature of the war the Chinese have prepared themselves to fight and examines the situation which the liberal democracies have put themselves into with decades of globalisation and accepting Chinese intrusions into their domestic economies and politics.

This is an important book and reflects the serious thinking and work which Babbage has devoted himself to over the past few years. One of the remedies which Babbage believes necessary to get the West into "fighting shape" is for the strategic leaderships in the West to discuss frankly with their publics all of the dimensions of the strategic challenge we now face. Babbage himself very much contributes to such leadership.

In my discussion with Babbage in April 2023, we focused on what he considers the three key elements to being able to shape broader defence capability. For Babbage, shaping a broader defence capability is not just about the ADF and its own operational capability. "If you're looking at it from Beijing's point of view, they'd have to think very carefully about messing with us for we do have a very capable although small military and we have even more powerful friends."

---

4. https://defense.info/book-review/2023/05/meeting-the-chine se-military-challenge-taking-the-wide-view/

But the ADF lacks strategic depth and sustainability. As Babbage noted: "We are in danger of being a one-month operational military in case of conflict due to the lack of economic and industrial depth, such as the provision of fuels and key munitions and spare parts."

The second aspect for Australia is its alliance structure. As Babbage underscored, Australia has focused upon ramping up its alliance working relationships to the point where its own forces can more effectively integrate with the Americans and are working towards greater cooperation with other allies as well, notably the Japanese.

The result is clear: "The sum of alliance efforts is greater than any of the parts. This is a consideration which Beijing has to realise is not working to its advantage. The Chinese threat has drawn many nations in the Pacific closer together to resist authoritarian interference."

And it is not just Pacific allies; a number of European states have woken up to the realisation that China directly threatens their interests, and they have to find ways to contribute to the deterrence of China as well. Babbage noted: "We will cooperate with a range of others, including a number of relatively powerful and capable Europeans with whom we have long-standing partnerships."

And that led to the discussion of the third element in Australian deterrence, developing more effective regional partnerships. Here, he discussed evolving relationships with India, Indonesia, and other Southeast Asian and South Pacific countries. Australia is working hard to develop closer military, security, economic, technological, and diplomatic relationships that can strengthen regional cooperation and deterrence.

Working with its neighbourhood much more directly and effectively is a key part of shaping the way ahead for Australia's deterrence strategy. But beyond these three key elements for shaping the way ahead for Australian deterrence, an important broader question is the need for national and alliance-wide efforts to strengthen strategic sustainability and endurance. We did not discuss this at length in this meeting, but it is the core of the analysis in his new book.

The challenge is to move from the near and midterm efforts at enhanced national military capability and allied interoperability to a stronger capability for resilient societies that empower enduring forces, not just one-month militaries. The core allies need to review and restructure their strategic supply chains as a matter of urgency to reinforce each other's economic and industrial strengths and cover their respective weaknesses.

New levels of allied cooperation are required along with new planning and management mechanisms. These initiatives are needed urgently if the allies are to have a credible deterrent going forward and if they are going to be able to endure and sustain themselves in the event of major conflict.

Chapter Seven

Sharpening the Edge

The Williams Foundation Seminar held on March 30, 2023, in Canberra was entitled "Sharpening the Edge of Australia's National Deterrence Capability," and it focused on the strategic transition of Australia and the ADF in meeting the challenges of the decade ahead.

The seminar itself was placed midway between two major government announcements about the changing approach to defence. The first was the announcement with regard to the way ahead with the generation of a new nuclear submarine capability for Australia and the second is the forthcoming release of the Defence Strategic Review, in late April 2023. The seminar took a broad view of the challenge of deterrence, that deterrent effects are not simply a result of what the ADF can do with its allies and partners but what the Australian polity, economy, culture, and society can deliver in competing with the twenty-first-century authoritarian powers and cooperate with allies going through a very fluid situation in their domestic polities, societies, cultures, and economies.

Australia and Deterrence in a Global System in Flux

The initial presentation to the seminar was by Air Marshal John Harvey (Retired). He has written a well-regarded assessment of deterrence published in 1997 and in his presentation, he looked back at that assessment as well as discussed the way ahead in the current decade. His presentation focused largely on establishing a baseline understanding of deterrence, and in a meeting with him in the week after the seminar, he discussed key challenges going forward.

Harvey noted that the most common definition of deterrence is the following: "the threatened use of force to convince an adversary 'not to do something.' There are three threat mechanisms on which deterrence is based: denial—where the aim is to defeat the aggressor's forces involved in the potential hostile action; retaliation—where the aim is to exact a proportionate cost from the aggressor without necessarily directly defeating the attacking forces; punishment—where the aim is to raise the cost of aggression through, for example, targeting the population of the aggressor force without necessarily targeting their military capability."

Harvey then identified three determinants of the success of deterrence: capability—the ability to carry out the threat on which the deterrent threat is based; credibility—whether or not there is seen to be commitment to carrying out the deterrent threat; communication—how effective the deterrer is in communicating the threat to the potential aggressor."

Harvey noted that deterrence is a means to an end, that it is "a tool at the service of policy." He went on to argue that "at best, deterrence is a stabilizing mechanism—it cannot remove the source of tension in an adversarial relationship. It may, however, be essential in stabilizing a situation such that diplomatic and political solutions can be found."

At the outset, Harvey stated that although the essentials of deterrence remained the same for Australia, there are significant changes since he wrote the book. On the one hand, there are changes in the means. He identified two: "the importance of the information domain and the emergence of cyberwarfare; and the increased importance of space to military operations and space as a future warfare domain." On the other hand, there is a major geopolitical shift: "the rise of China as a major military power across all warfare domains, including nuclear weapons." If we add to this the significant shift in the alliance structure along with the adversarial set of challenges, the magnitude of the shift can be seen in terms of the deterrent challenge facing Australia.

As the chief of Army, Lieutenant General Simon Stuart put it in his presentation: "Pax-Americana was a historic anomaly. The norm in human history is a violent transfer of power from one empire to another—and 14 of the 16 transitions between empires in human history have involved wars. We live in an era that might be described as post-peak globalisation. Understanding how the international system works, what the great economic or trading blocks are, is an endeavour we need to understand."

I would add that understanding China as an adversary is a major task all on its own. We have a younger generation who grew up as beneficiaries of the Chinese way of playing globalisation. Why are they now an adversary?

China and Russia have operated within our societies in ways the Soviet Union could only dream of doing. A great term which captured this reality is the term Londongrad in describing Britain and its relationship with Russia up to the Ukraine War. Similar realities exist in the United States and Australia concerning the degree of Chinese involvement in our domestic lives.

And the significant deterrence history we generated in the 1980s is more a historical museum than a set of experiences to be learned from. And when you add to that the state of our knowledge of our authoritarian competitors and how their leaders define risk assessment and knowing what deters them, we face a real challenge. You cannot rely on funding from Confucius Institutes to train our own analytical capability on the nature of our competitors.

This means that shaping effective deterrence and practising the art of statecraft for Australia and its allies in a world in flux will be difficult, challenging, and not easily achieved. When I talked with Air Marshal Harvey (Retired) the week following the seminar, he underscored the challenging nature of the transition.

In our discussion, Harvey underscored that what was required in the new context was a whole of government, society, and whole of alliance capability. With regard to mobilisation, he made the very sound point that mobilisation was important across the whole of government and society to deal with a variety of challenges, not just defence. Indeed, if one correlated mobilisation simply with defence, that would lead to failure to focus on the much broader challenge which is best characterised by a capability for national resilience. From this point of view, deterrence then is based on social cohesion and national cohesion to sustain Australia through the pressures which the changing global system puts upon her.

The presentation by Secretary Michael Pezzullo of the Department of Home Affairs at the seminar indeed focused specifically on this question of the broader question of national resilience which was of enhanced importance in the new phases of Australian defence. Pezzullo focused largely on the experience of Australia in World War II when the country was slow to respond to the threat but over time became mobilised to in fact deal with the challenges. Pezzullo cited Brendan Sargeant's work on strategic imagination to make the point that "our capacity to envisage and prepare for the future is a function of the limits of our strategic imagination. The effective exercise of strategic imagination in the 1930s would have seen a better prepared and more resilient Australia."

Pezzullo then noted: "Strategies are tasked with conceptual as well as particulars, different strategic assumptions, policy settings and operational capabilities, Australia's part would have generated different risk calculations for Japan. Amongst other things Australia should have adapted a geographically focused strategy, which would have dictated the building of a different military force based around an air defence system across the north of Australia, a long-range bomber force, a larger army and a land force which was able to deploy to the Australian territories and Papua and New Guinea, across northern Australia and potentially into our new littoral region."

Pezzullo concluded: "My thesis is in terms of resilience and deterrence; democracies will always be slow to start. Because we don't focus on war. We don't focus on conquest. And we don't focus on the totalitarian aggregation of all functions of states around a single leader, around a single ideology for a single program. We live our lives. So we're slow to stand, because we live freely. My contention is that history teaches us that we finish more strongly. And why is that? As you've seen that today in the Ukraine, the mobilization of consent is by popular will and organic and is not dictated and a ferocity that can overcome any tyrant and that is perhaps the ultimate deterrent."

Clearly, we have now entered such a tine. How will the art of statecraft be combined with the enhanced deterrent effect of the ADF and allied military forces? If we look back at Sargeant's essay referred to earlier, a number of the key challenges facing Australia and its allies are underscored: "Two decades of ADF deployments to the Middle East and Afghanistan has built operational capability but perhaps at the cost of narrowing our ability to think strategically about our interests. This has been recognized, and recent policy statements such as the Defence Strategic Update 2020 have begun a process of reorientation to the Indo-Pacific as the area of our primary strategic concern. There have been the beginnings of an outreach towards other strategic relationships in our region, notably Japan and India, though this work is slow and will be very challenging.

"We have struggled to develop a confident position in relation to China, and we have perhaps been more optimistic than we should have been about China's strategic ambition. This argues for a much more agile policy and a much more aggressive approach to the construction and management of our strategic interests. Others have framed this in terms of a stronger, more geographically centred regional focus in our policy and activity that might manifest itself in a much greater engagement with Indonesia and other South East Asian countries.

"I agree with this approach, but I would frame it also in terms of a much richer imaginative engagement with the Indo-Pacific more broadly, with a recognition that even as we have our own distinctive Australian identity, we are part of this community, and that the nature of the community also shapes our identity and the way in which we might live in this world. Such an imaginative engagement might lead us to see what we might learn from the strategic traditions across the many Indo Pacific countries if we allow them to challenge our strategic imagination.

"We might also question why, as a community, we have in recent years made border protection the overriding policy and institutional imperative for the construction of our national security system, when the much larger and more strategically pressing issue is how we engage with the Indo-Pacific during a period of major change to the global strategic order? We might ask whether this preoccupation with the border constitutes the major contemporary failure of our strategic imagination . . .

"The work of policy, an art of desire, is to say what the world might be. The work of strategy is to create the path towards that world, responding to all the known and unknown impediments that are likely to emerge. Policy lives mostly in the world of imagination; strategy lives mostly in the world of experience. The art of the policy maker and the strategist is to bring imagination into the world of experience and through this to create strategy that can change the world. In times of great change, the challenge is to imagination, for continuity in strategy is likely to lead to failure. Sir Arthur Tange, an important figure in Australian foreign and defence policy making and strategy, once said that strategy without resources is no strategy.

"In my professional life those words were a touchstone. My argument now is that as we learn to live in the Indo-Pacific, strategy without imagination is sterile."

Shaping a Nuclear Submarine Enterprise in Australia

In March 2020, I was visiting Western Australia, including HMAS Sterling. I was there to visit the HMAS Rankin, one of the Collins class submarines home-ported at HMAS Sterling on Garden Island.

When I informed a senior U.S. Navy Admiral that I was going to visit the Royal Australian Navy at Garden Island, he wrote: "Awesome, say hello to the fellas down south, incredible team! And absolutely critical in/out of a fight."

Little did I know at the time of my visit which was 12 March 2020, that in fact I was visiting a future SSN base. I also did not know that I was about to have to escape Australia to get back to the United States with the onset of the pandemic.

In my visits to Australia during the period when Australia was working with France on the build of a new generation diesel-powered submarine, my work with the U.S. Navy, my time in France at my Paris apartment and discussions with the French, and my discussions in Australia gave me a good view of progress on this program. Then in September 2021, while in my apartment in Paris, the Australian, British, and American governments announced that Australia was to cancel the French program in favour of an SSN program which would involve the three countries, or the Anglo-Saxons as the French refer to the three, although it is difficult to view the United States or the United Kingdom in this light as the two countries change significantly. Being in France, I certainly had a chance to talk with the French and with colleagues in the United States. I could do so by phone and video, and of course reached out to Australian colleagues to sort out an initial read on all of this as well.

I wrote several pieces on this development at the time, but not surprisingly, the most perceptive of the pieces was built around an interview with Vice-Admiral Tim Barrett (Retired). This is what I wrote in a piece published on 19 October 2021: "During my visit to Europe earlier this Fall, the surprise announcement of the Morrison Administration's decision to shift from their French alliance to deliver a long-range diesel submarine to acquiring nuclear submarine capability through an alliance with the United States and Britain was made. I talked with both French and Australian analysts and provided my initial assessment in a series of articles which highlighted the decision and the dynamics of change associated with that decision.

"But what was clear that the strategic environment has changed dramatically from when the Australian government made its decision to stay with a conventional submarine capability. The nature of the Chinese threat as well as the actions of the Xi Administration has clearly driven a shift in Australian thinking and perceived needs for longer range operational capability in the Indo-Pacific region.

"At the same time, its closest allies in the region the United States and Japan clearly recognize the need to expand their capabilities to operate throughout the region to complicate Chinese operational considerations, and to deter via more capability to operate throughout the wider Pacific as well.

"The announced decision highlighted an 18-month period with Vice Admiral Jonathan Mead in charge on the Australian side of negotiating within the new nuclear submarine alliance to deliver Australian solutions. I interviewed Mead when he was head of Navy Capability in 2016. He then went on to be Commander Australian Fleet and then Chief of Joint Capabilities and Command of Joint Capabilities Group. He has a strong ASW background as well as working closely with the other member of the Quad, namely India. He is now the Chief of the Nuclear-Powered Submarine Task Force . . .

"I had a chance to discuss these issues on October 14, 2021, in a phone interview with Vice-Admiral (Retired) Tim Barrett, with whom I have had the opportunity to discuss maritime issues since 2015. As the exact nature of what will happen in the program is a work in progress and not really open to public disclosure until that

18-month period is completed, we focused on the context and how one might assess that context.

"Vice-Admiral (Retired) Barrett made three key points. First, the nuclear submarine effort was a strategic one, which was about Australian defence and not primarily focused on a priority on ship building on Australian soil. It is crucial to understand that this is about adding core defence capabilities earlier rather than later and would almost certainly encompass interaction between shaping the eco system for the operation of Australian nuclear submarines and the presence of allied nuclear submarines working with the Australian eco system.

"The second key point was that the priority needed to be focused on adding nuclear submarine capability to the evolving USW or ASW capability which Australia was already building out. The Australian government recently decided to add another squadron of Romeo helicopters to the fleet and has procured P-8s and Tritons as part of an expanded ASW or USW warfighting capability. The submarine is not a silver bullet for ASW or USW mission sets but part of the evolution of the kill web approach to ASW and USW missions going forward .
. .

"According to Barrett: 'The submarine decision is part of a broader set of decisions with regard to how the ADF should respond to the challenges in the Indo-Pacific. This was a deliberate and considered position from the Navy's perspective, but the political and geopolitical circumstances have changed. This is not the first time that Australia has sought or considered the acquisition of a nuclear submarine.'

"The third key point was that flexibility and innovations will be part of working out a way ahead and he noted that Mead had worked with him previously. When Commander of the Australian Fleet, then Commodore Mead was instrumental in working an innovative plan to manage a temporary capability deficiency for fleet fuel tanking. To shore up a gap, the RAN 'leased' a Spanish Navy oiler for 8 months, and the RAN crews trained on the ship and operated the ship in support of the Australian Fleet.

"Eventually, the RAN acquired two new Spanish oilers, but the kind of innovation demonstrated in this example, will almost certainly be part of the way ahead in meeting the challenges of accelerating the operational acquisition of nuclear submarine capacity in support of Australian defence.

"According to Vice Admiral (Retired) Barrett: 'The strategic environment has changed. We need to reconsider the balance between sovereign capability for a thirty-year build and the need for creation of capability in the near term. The earlier 30-year period build approach should not be the dominant approach; the capability and its presence to shape deterrent capabilities is crucial and work out over time how the build side of this effort is clarified and put in place. The program needs to be driven by the need for creative capability options first.'[1]

Now after the 18-month period, the three countries announced their joint decision on how to proceed on the Australian approach to acquire nuclear attack submarine technology and capability. To do so, will require Australia to build a comprehensive enterprise to operate, maintain, to sustain, and build an Australian nuclear attack submarine.

The comprehensive approach to do so was announced in mid-March 2023 in San Diego by the three heads of state. The Williams Seminar was held on 30 March 2023 and is sandwiched be-

---

1. https://sldinfo.com/2021/10/shaping-a-way-ahead-for-the-aust ralian-submarine-capability-the-perspective-of-vice-admiral-reti red-barrett/

tween this event and the public release of the strategic defence review in late April 2023.

The Australian government released a report laying out how it saw the "partnership for the future" or "the AUKUS nuclear-powered submarine pathway." In that report, the government described the advantage of nuclear-powered submarines and why Australia was transitioning to an SSN capability. "In the future security environment of the Indo-Pacific, conventionally powered submarines will be increasingly less able to meet Australia's needs. The United Kingdom Royal Navy and United States Navy retired their last conventionally powered submarines in the early 1990s because SSNs have superior stealth, speed, manoeuvrability, survivability and endurance when compared to diesel-electric powered submarines."[2]

At the Williams Seminar, Vice-Admiral Mead provided an overview to the approach being taken to establish a nuclear submarine enterprise in Australia. In essence, the approach is three-fold. In the first phase, UK and U.S. nuclear submarines will visit HMAS Stirling, and the Royal Australian Navy will learn how to support these ships during their visits. As part of this stand-up phase, Australia will work with the United States in operating Virginia class submarines. In the second phase, Australia will obtain Virginia class submarines and operate anywhere from three to five of these boats going forward. And in a third phase, Australia will particulate with its partners in shaping a new class of SSNs, which will be British designed but enabled by U.S. technologies. In this third phase, Australia will have built its own submarine yard at Osborne where, in effect, this would be the fourth nuclear submarine yard in the trilateral alliance. In other words, the

---

2. https://www.defence.gov.au/about/taskforces/aukus

notion of building an arsenal of democracy through allied cooperation would be realised.

Vice-Admiral Mead started his presentation by indicating that "in 2027, the U.S. will forward rotate Virginia class submarines to Australia and the UK would rotate one nuclear submarine to HMAS Sterling. The aim of this effort will be to allow Australia to deeply immerse itself in a nuclear-powered program. We will be doing maintenance on Virginia class submarines and will be doing crewing of these submarines out of Western Australia. After a period of about four or five years, we will reach the point where our partners and we will be able to ensure that Australia is a safe and secure steward of nuclear technology, of nuclear materials and nuclear reactors. From that point in time, the United States would offer us for sale or transfer up to five Virginia class submarines."

This would constitute the stand-up and launch phase for Australia shaping a nuclear submarine exercise, and really the key one to ensure a capability being able to operate to replace the Collins class submarines. This is really the key effort which enables the threshold to be crossed into a period of operating nuclear submarines.

In my view, this also allows Australia to build its con-ops for integrated USW and ASW with the P-8s, Tritons, and various air and maritime assets, including the coming of maritime autonomous systems to build an integrated offensive-defensive capability to protect Australian sea lanes.

What then follows is working through what a follow-on submarine program would look like. And this effort will entail in depth cooperation with both the United Kingdom and the United States. According to Mead: "It will be a follow-on to the British nuclear-powered submarine but will incorporate U.S. technology, including weapons, sensors, VLS combat systems and torpedoes."

Vice-Admiral Mead then looked beyond the pathway discussion to the broader question of what Australia needs to do for this effort to be successful. The first element is addressing the strategy and being able to gain support for the effort within the Australian public. "We are going to have to be very clear on our strategy." Second, Australia must successfully manage the trilateral working relationship. "How can we make the best of Australia working with the U.S. and the UK to deliver this capability?" Third, creating, training, and sustaining the appropriate workforce for the enterprise is a major challenge within Australia. "We will be the first country in the world to operate a nuclear submarine without having a civilian nuclear industry. This presents some unique challenges." Fourth, Australia needs to build the appropriate infrastructure both in terms of basing and in terms of the shipyard itself. There will be some unique aspects to the yard, including shaping high security protection for the yard as well. "We need to design the yard, build the yard and start building the nuclear-powered submarine by the end of the decade." Fifth, Australia needs to build an industrial base for this effort which can support and sustain the effort into the indefinite future. Osborne will become the fourth nuclear submarine yard to go with the two in the United States and the one in the United Kingdom. "Osborne will become one of the most advanced and complex technological hubs in the world." Sixth, the security of the enterprise is a major element for success. In addition to the physical security mentioned earlier, the IAEA involvement will be significant in verifying the quality of Australian nuclear power stewardship. "If we don't have the international community along with us, the enterprise will fail."

But the point of all this effort was highlighted by Vice-Admiral Mead at the beginning of his presentation: "There is no more powerful instrument of conventional deterrence than a nuclear-powered submarine capability."

The Perspective of Air Marshal Chipman, RAAF

How can Australia as a middle power deter a major power like China from the use of force against Australia and undercutting Australian interests and way of life? This is a challenging question to pose as the world is changing significantly in the post-pandemic era and with it, the evolution of the relationship among authoritarian powers and the dynamics of change within the liberal democratic allies of Australia as well. The technologies of war are in the process of significant change, although the basics of war and conflict persist.

At the seminar, Air Marshal Chipman provided his perspective on how the ADF and the RAAF will evolve with the deterrent challenge in the evolving context. His focus was upon deterrence from the perspective of a middle power and its ability to deliver a deterrent effect.

At one point in his presentation, he highlighted a way to understand deterrence. "Admiral Harry Harris, the former Commander of INDOPACOM, explained deterrence with a simple mathematical equation: deterrence = capability + resolve + signalling. If anyone of these is zero, then the product, deterrence, is zero! Resolve and signalling are orchestrated through diplomacy, but they are underpinned by military capability. We influence the calculus of our potential adversaries in all that we do. Force generation is not just the act of preparing for war, it also signals our preparedness for war, and therefore serves to deter it. We should think strategically about our force generation signalling."

If we examine these three aspects—capability, resolve, and signalling—we can look at Chipman's presentation in terms of how he dealt with each of these elements of deterrence.

Capability

The question of capability must be determined in relationship to whom you are trying to deter. Given the growing capability of our authoritarian adversaries for precision strike and magazine depth, we have focused on greater ability to disperse or disaggregate force and to work ways to integrate the effects of that force. This is what I have underscored as the shaping of a kill-web force.

Chipman emphasised in his presentation several aspects of this trajectory of change. "We are also sharpening our deterrence capability by strengthening our resilience to military coercion and intimidation. A resilient Middle Power will minimise the consequences of adversary actions, through passive measures such as hardening, deception and dispersal. And by refining our agile fighting concepts to manoeuvre across our network of northern bases, through all domains, complicating and obscuring the adversaries' targeting options. "Active measures that protect critical infrastructure and vulnerable supply lines, that strengthen our national resilience, will also help convince potential adversaries of the futility of their action."

Working air assets with ground and sea assets to deliver a combined effect, often referred to as multi-domain effects, is a key focus of attention for the RAAF as well. As Chipman put it: "We have successfully transitioned to the F-35, with its world-leading ability to achieve surprise, gain access, sense and share targetable data, and deliver lethal effects both in offence and in defence. "Integrated with the Super Hornet, Growler and E-7A Wedgetail, our air combat team is formidable. And they're ready. We test them regularly, through exercises such as TASMAN SHIELD, which recently teamed our full air combat system with two Air Warfare Destroyers to practice high-end, integrated, multi-domain warfare. We are investing in long-range weapon systems, capable of striking well-defended warships on the move at great range from Australia. This will be an important complement to our maritime and land forces. Together, we'll present a complex, integrated, multi-domain challenge for potential adversaries to penetrate."

Resolve

With regard to resolve, the challenge is for deterrence to be a whole of government and whole of society effort. This is hard, particularly after the land wars which have largely been experienced as a boutique military engagement. This will require taking serious looks and change with regard to economic and cultural relationships with China, sharpening realistic energy policies, shaping cyber and information resilience at home, and other macro-economic changes far beyond the ability of the ADF to generate.

Chipman did not speak to these aspects of resolve in any depth but focused on what resolve meant in terms of the ADF itself. Chipman spoke to the general issues of resolve in these terms: "It is also in our strategic culture to stand defiant when subject to coercion or intimidation. There is a role for deterrence here, through our readiness, resilience and the resourcefulness of our people. We generate combat power, integrated across domains, in pursuit of our national objectives, for the purpose of preventing conflict. But we remain resolute to act if our deterrence strategy fails."

He referred to the skill and initiative of the men and women who make up the ADF. He argued that if they are to operate a kill web force successfully, the ADF will need to have creative and capable warriors who can operate effectively at the tactical edge led by senior leaders not pre-occupied by micro-management.

And Chipman's counterpart, the PACAF Commander General Wilsbach, underscored the growing impact which integrated deterrence can have on the authoritarian powers. The ability of the allied forces to work effectively together within a crisis setting enhances the deterrent power of any member of the coalition, but certainly scales up the potential impact of a middle power. An effective middle power must master "coalitionability."

As the Colonel and now Major General Anders Rex of Denmark put in our seminar held in 2015 in Copenhagen: "Col. Anders Rex, Chief of the Expeditionary Air Staff of the Danish Air Force, coined a phrase 'coalitionability' to express his focus on the core requirement of allied air forces and defence forces shaping ways to work more effectively with one another in dealing with twenty-first century cha llenges."[3]

As Air Marshal Chipman put it: "Our capability and willingness to stand alongside allies and likeminded partners—with combined diplomatic and military weight. Our readiness to act in unison, with political and strategic alignment underpinned by technical, procedural and human interoperability. The threat of responding as an alliance will exacerbate a fear to attack and strengthen our deterrence capability."

Chipman went on to enhance those comments: "It is surely the central pillar of a Middle Power deterrence strategy—to operate in concert with allies and partners in pursuit of common interests. To deter other nations from acting against those interests by presenting strength in numbers, wherever and whenever that is demanded of us. This is not about surrendering sovereignty, but rather sharing it

---

3. https://sldinfo.com/2015/04/coalition-operations-are-in-the-da nish-dna-finding-the-gold-in-coalitions/

among trusted allies and partners—to advance our national interest. This is the experience of our alliance relationship with the United States for over 70 years. But of course, this strategy extends beyond the United States. Through training, education, key leadership engagement, development assistance and crisis response. Building partner capacity, strengthening our partner's sovereignty will help inoculate our region from the predations of others."

Signalling

Now let us turn to signalling. This is a key aspect of deterrence but a neglected one during the land wars. It is a forgotten art. In the 1980s, much of my work in Europe and with the Russians during the Euro-missile crisis and then the run up to what would become the unification of Germany was in the domain of communication and signalling. We only avoided nuclear war in 1983 by activating communication and signalling networks.

How are we going to do that today? How do we do so with the Chinese? The Russians? The North Koreans? All three are Pacific powers and will shape the play of conflict in the region.

Air Marshal Chipman in his presentation focused on the central significance of thinking through how the adversary might think in a crisis and to calibrate our messages to do so. Messaging obviously comes through actions as well as words, but both are important. This is how he put it: "Imagine you are a leader of one of the most powerful nations on earth—with deep financial resources, extraordinary industrial capacity and an impressive military capability. Power, prosperity, longevity pull on all three strings of Thucydides' famous triptych—fear, honour, interest. From your vantage point, advantage is easily accrued or coerced. What cannot be coerced can ultimately be compelled. What has long been coveted can now be imagined and may even be within your reach. How might your ambitions be deterred?

What might make you fear to attack? A rational leader might start with a cost-benefit judgement. Relative interest and relative power are the core ingredients that will shape this judgement. How important is this interest? Is it a core interest or peripheral to your national objectives? How do your interests intersect the interests of others? How determined, committed, or desperate will they be to defend them? What is your military advantage—in technical and numerical terms; your strategic reserve and capacity to absorb counter actions; what about your experience, resolve, fighting spirit? Is your force as capable as you believe it to be? Recent expeditions in Europe might give pause to ponder. Is your adversary concealing strengths? Will they escalate in ways you can't anticipate? Will they mobilise allies and partners against you?

"These uncertainties will play on your judgement in a military sense, as will relative economic power and international legitimacy. The potential these challenges might present across all operational domains and elements of national power simultaneously, must in itself influence your thinking. Surely, for a rational actor, doubt lingers . . . How might you control your destiny if you choose a path of uncertainty?"

He concluded his presentation with some general observations about what one might call "the practice" of deterrence or what I would call the ability to operate your military force within the general context of the art of statecraft, which, in my view, seems a lost art. "Let me finish on a cautionary note. I mentioned earlier that deterrence works on the threat of escalation. But we must be clear, as a Middle Power, this must stop short of actually provoking conflict. Deterrence fails at the point conflict begins.

"Strategic competition is dynamic and unstable: peripheral interests might become core over time. For a deterrence strategy to succeed through a prolonged period of strategic competition, we must also build pathways for de-escalation. This is as important in force design and force posture as it is to campaign design. The capabilities we invest in, where we stage them and how we intend to use them.

"De-escalation pathways restore the pre-crisis or pre-conflict balance of power. Seizing a diplomatic off-ramp too early may cede advantage; too late will cause unnecessary attrition. Our successful deterrence strategy will need to consider escalation and de-escalation in equal measure.

"So let me conclude. Our Middle Power deterrence capability is fixed by relative interest and relative power dynamics. Where a potential adversary's core interests are at stake, deterrence requires strength, and strength comes in numbers. It is axiomatic of Australia's strategic culture, that we seek to work with allies and partners in defence of our common interests, and this will endure.

"Which takes us back once again to the mind of our potential adversaries. To ensure they understand our core interests, and interpret our signals accurately, so that we might compete, deter and de-escalate without provoking conflict."

The Perspective of Lieutenant General Simon Stuart, Australian Army

With the Australian Army having been heavily invested in the Middle East land wars and working closely with the U.S. Army in those endeavours, what is the Australian Army's role in the enhanced emphasis on the direct defence of Australia? Of course, each of the services and the joint force itself is facing how to meet the challenge of direct defence, but the question of the relationship of the land forces to the joint direct defence of Australia is especially challenging.

Lieutenant General Simon Stuart, Chief of Staff of the Australian Army, provided a general look at the deterrence challenge, the role of the ADF and of the Australian Army in his presentation at the seminar. With the emergence of what is often called great power competition, the role of the nation has been enhanced even when integration with key allies is central to the way ahead for national deterrence.

Lieutenant General Stuart then addressed the question of an Australian approach from that perspective: "If there were to be such a thing as a uniquely Australian way of deterring, it would surely be founded by what defines us as a nation and what defines us Australians. "Who are we as a nation, and who are we as a people in the middle decades of the twenty-first century? A uniquely Australian approach to deterrence would surely be founded in what our national aspirations were, our strategic culture, and approaching the task of deterrence from that perspective. So, the founding question for me is: how do we conceive of and combine our amazing national endowment? Our enviable strategic geography, our stewardship of a significant proportion of the Earth's surface—both the land mass and the seas that we are responsible for, and over 40 percent of the Antarctic continent, which we lay claim to.

"We are among the world's top 15 economies, we have convening power both regionally and globally, we have a vibrant and diverse successful social experiment in our society today, our amazing human capital, and we have a series and a set of alliances and partnerships which are the envy of many. We have the capacity to be a global energy and food superpower. We have incredible natural resources, both those that have been in demand up until now, and those that will be in demand in the future. And the capacity to draw on 65,000 years of human history and endeavour on our continent.

"So how can we conceive of that wonderful endowment, and how do we conceive bringing it together? Are we outwardly focused and engaged, or are we insular and closed? And, for everyone who wears or has worn our uniform today—and certainly for every Australian soldier—the answer to the question 'who are we?' is of fundamental importance to service. Because we need to understand for whom and for what we are serving. And if we are in the fight, those questions are brought into even sharper relief.

Lieutenant General Stuart then addressed the key question of the nature of the new strategic context within which Australia or other liberal democracies are now operating.

"Pax-Americana was a historic anomaly. The norm in human history is a violent transfer of power from one empire to another—and 14 of the 16 transitions between empires in human history have involved wars. We live in an era that might be described as post-peak globalisation. Understanding how the international system works, what the great economic or trading blocks are, is an endeavour we need to understand.

"There are a range of theories, but personally I like Parag Khanna's new regionalism model because it emphasises partnerships, and partnerships within the context of regional blocks from an economic perspective—but also from the other elements of national power, which are in the ascendancy in the global system today.

"To some of our more recent history and the thinking from the 1980s that shaped our national security and defence policy, strategy and practice over the last 30 years. The thinking that we do today, and the decisions that our elected representatives make today, will influence our policy and practice over the next few decades. That thinking, in my view, failed to engage with the world as it was, failed to engage with globalisation, either refused to engage or didn't recognise pretty much everything we've actually been doing these past few decades. It was defensive and inward looking.

"And finally, the wars we've been involved in, the wars we've been fighting over the last 20 years, the so-called 'wars of choice,' did not touch Australia and did not touch Australians. They were a defence endeavour, involving only the military element of our national power, and largely an ADF endeavour. They did not touch the society we live in."

What then shapes a way ahead for the ADF in this new historical era is the importance of being embedded in a broader national approach requiring skill sets beyond those expected of the military. Lieutenant General Stuart then addressed some of these broader capabilities. "How does our national aspiration and our national identity find expression in our strategic thinking and our policy and practice. It finds expression via statecraft, which is the mobilisation and orchestration of all elements of national power.

"And the key areas of focus are that people like us need to help our elected representatives deal with are founded in national identity, and national unity, and therefore the wellspring of unity and purpose. It relies on social cohesion. It relies on the means by which to execute the strategy—that is our economy—the means connote and provide agency for us as a nation. It will rely on an involved relationship between the private and public sector, on better harnessing the incredible capacity of our academy. It will rely on the practice of statecraft on a more expansive engagement with partners and the development of partnerships."

Lieutenant General Stuart finally focused on the military element of deterrence. "The military element of national power needs to be four things. Firstly, it needs to reflect our national identity and aspiration. It needs to reflect the nature of the challenges, the threats and the competition. And it needs to reflect the nature of our strategy, which in its broadest terms is shape, deter and respond. It needs to respect the arc of human history, and the history of warfare, and respect the requirement to balance between the enduring human nature of warfare and its changing character—which is generally speaking dominated by technology. It needs to ensure relevance—relevance and credibility that are relative to a pacing threat, and an operating environment, and the opinions of our allies and partners. It also needs to be resourced because a strategy without means is an illusion.

"So our strategy today calls on us to shape the environment, deter actions against our interests, and be ready to respond with military force in all five domains when required. But shape, deter and respond does not connote a linear progression or the luxury of focusing on one at the expense of others. It is all three, all at once and in five domains, in the context of the execution and application of statecraft. If deterrence fails, war and its very unpredictability demands an ADF that is relevant and credible in all five domains—a system of systems that has the best chance of mission success whether we are deterring or we are prevailing in the conquest of war.

"To come back to the point about strategy being an illusion if it is not resourced, there are key questions that are being asked today in our nation. "We have a pretty good sense of what it costs. There is a sharp focus on what we can afford, and then there are choices about what we are willing to pay. Each of those price points brings with it a risk profile, and those are the difficult decisions that our government needs to make. Those are difficult decisions to which we need to contribute the best advice that we possibly can."

Lieutenant General Stuart then focused on the way ahead for the ADF and the Army. "Given the nature of our strategic circumstances, whatever we do requires us to do it quickly. Velocity matters. "One way we can sharpen the edge of deterrence is by embracing new and emerging technologies and balancing that with the incredible human capital we enjoy in our country.

"I'm going to quote our Chief of Air Force from his excellent speech, which I commend to you, which he gave as a keynote at the Chief of Air Force Symposium in Melbourne as a precursor to the Avalon Air Show recently. He said: 'It is easy to be seduced by technology; to do so would be to forget that national security is a national endeavour. The impediments to boosting capability delivery are often policy related, procedural or cultural. While advanced platforms teamed with cutting edge and disruptive technologies can be game-changes, we won't realise their advantage without evolving our thinking that delivers the military power element of deterrence.'

"I think for me that really summarised the set of dilemmas and choices we face today in terms of responding to the strategic environment.

"Another way forward is leveraging the existing strengths of our Defence Force by ensuring we have a sharper focus on how we design our force, which is integrated and greater than the sum of our constituent parts. One that increasingly builds into the architecture a strong and abiding sense of partnership with allies and regional partners. Because in an era of great power competition, having more friends is better than having less. In our region we have very good relationships with our partners. And the people-to-people relationships we enjoy have been grown and cultivated and reinforced over many, many years and stand us well for the future.

"Shared interests matter, and the many collective agreements like AUKUS and like FPDA and the Quad, and like the support we have of the ASEAN political architecture matter and stand us in good stead for tomorrow.

"From an Army perspective, from the contribution of land power to that integrated force, we offer presence, persistence, asymmetry through first-mover advantage, utility, and incredibly good value for money."

How Detection Is a Key Part of the Deterrence Effort

Jake Campbell, Triton program director, Northrop Grumman Australia, highlighted one area within a deterrence strategy, namely how detection can enable various deterrent actions.

Campbell is an experienced RAAF officer with many years of experience in the ISR area. I first met Jake when he had been appointed along with the current chief of the RAAF as the co-heads of Jericho.[4] Their initial focus was very much in line with Jake's current work on Triton and his thoughts on "deterrence by detection."

He started his presentation by highlighting his focus as follows: How does Australia's detection capabilities contribute to the overall deterrence package?

His answer was that it depends on where and how that capability was exercised by the operational forces and I would add the ability of

---

4. https://sldinfo.com/2015/09/the-co-directors-of-plan-jericho-group-captain-rob-chipman-and-group-captain-jake-campbell-discuss-the-way-ahead-for-the-raaf/

the political authorities who are working with the operational forces to get the deterrent effect. Put in other terms, it is the challenge of having the right military tool kit combined with the practice of the art of statecraft.

Campbell argued that "deterrence can only be successful with a clearly defined and communicated outcome and with the ability to use a carefully balanced mix of necessary options to deliver that outcome. What we are really talking about is deterrence by design." With this laydown of the concept of deterrence, he then highlighted the perspective of one analyst which emphasised the following: "Adversaries are less likely to commit opportunistic acts of aggression if they know they are being watched constantly and that their actions can be publicized widely." Detection is part of the deterrence package but for it to work as such, it must be linked to capabilities for credible action and there needs to be a track record of a state actually responding in an appropriate manner to a threat once detected.

This is how Campbell characterised the above point: "Deterrence is only possible and effective if Australia has a clearly defined and communicated deterrence outcome." Campbell cautioned that "deterrence by detection only works if it is linked to a credible deterrence response option, and a willingness to respond on order to deliver a combined deterrence effect.

He expanded on that point as follows: "What is Australia's balance of interests that drive the deterrence outcomes? And ultimately what is Australia deterring? Is it an attack on Australia? Our sea lines of communication? Is it our offshore network infrastructure, our critical onshore infrastructure? Is it an attack on our region? Whether that's the Southwest Pacific or Southeast Asia or law of the sea, or an attack on our allies? Are we trying to deter an attack on Taiwan? Are we trying to deter a superior adversary, a near pear adversary or a rudimentary adversary?"

Campbell argued that when focused on deterrence by detection, the role of layered ISR changes in the various operational phases of what one might consider a deterrent process or perhaps continuum. He put his assessment this way: "While deterrence by detection can deliver strategic effects, deterrence is also effective in phase zero and phase one operation by leveraging quality ISR information when carefully coordinated with the public and classified use of that information.

"In early phases, the full force of diplomatic, economic, and public information efforts can be brought to bear. Once combat operations have commenced, the scope of those options are significantly reduced and the effectiveness of deterrence by detection is clearly significantly reduced. Detection operations can serve to suppress the effectiveness of grey zone operations by enabling public and international community awareness. And when necessary, the ability to use non-military responses."

He warned that "there is a risk that we will collect too much, or low fidelity data. To be effective Australia and our allies need better ways to turn the collected data into actionable intelligence . . .

"And there is a risk that the intelligence community won't make the important information public. Balancing the need to protect versus the need to create deterrence will be challenging, but we need to do so for deterrence to be effective."

In his assessment, Australia is building out the kind of layered ISR capability necessary for the art of deterrence by detection. He underscored that "critically layered ISR must be backed by a responsive sophisticated intelligence capability that can exploit the ISR product quickly to enable selective public release of information and shine a light on aggressive grey zone tactics or conventional force posture changes."

Campbell concluded that the evolution of layered ISR and its role in deterrence was a key area for industrial-government collaboration, cooperation, and successful delivery of ongoing capabilities. "Deterrence will depend in part upon industry's ability to field advanced sensors and platforms quickly and efficiently. Digital engineering has much to offer here. But we also need to find better ways to rapidly reconstitute capabilities.

"And I'm not just talking about low end capabilities; we need to be able to reconstitute our high-end capabilities quickly. Industry also has a role in making the ISR layers more robust through new concepts for ISR, backed by resilient communications pathways. And I encourage defence and the services to include industry as you start to develop new thinking."

Turning Point

After the seminar, I asked one of the young officers who attended the seminar what they got out of the seminar: "We are facing a significant strategic shift and those of us just now in service need to understand what the focus of the defence of our country is and will need to be as we work to defend our country."

Another young officer said: "The last generation fought abroad; now we are defending our country and in our region. How are we going to do so effectively?"

This was rather nicely put, as the ADF and Australia as a nation with regard to its defence is at a historical turning point.

Chapter Eight

The Defence Strategic Review

At the end of April 2023, the Australian government released its defence strategic review (DSR).[1] The documents and the presentations by government underscore that this effort is to lead to significant change for the ADF and the nation in dealing with the evolving Australia's strategic environment.

Nonetheless. there is a gap between resourcing and statement of intentionality with no new funding forthcoming associated with the strategic review. This leaves unresolved major questions about the future of the ADF and the nation's broader response to the Chinese challenge, in spite of the encouraging words in the DSR itself. But I have always believed that briefing charts about defence only kill the audience, not build systems that kill the enemy. So words are nice but

---

1. https://www.defence.gov.au/about/reviews-inquiries/defence
   -strategic-review

concrete, realistic, viable capabilities are much better when considering the nation's defence needs.

The DSR

The review is very clear about the altered circumstances facing Australia. "Australia's region, the Indo-Pacific, faces increasing competition that operates on multiple levels – economic, military, strategic and diplomatic – all interwoven and all framed by an intense contest of values and narratives. A large-scale conventional and non-conventional military build-up without strategic reassurance is contributing to the most challenging circumstances in our region for decades. Combined with rising tensions and reduced warning time for conflict, the risks of military escalation or miscalculation are rising."

To meet new strategic challenges, requires the ADF to operate further from Australia within the Indo-Pac region. "The ADF must have the capacity to engage in impactful projection across the full spectrum of proportionate response. The ADF must be able to hold an adversary at risk further from our shores."

To do so, the ADF must have a "fully integrated and more capable ADF."

The review indicated what is viewed as "immediate" actions to "reprioritise Defence's capabilities in line with the review's recommendations."

These are identified as follows:

- "investing in conventionally-armed, nuclear-powered submarines through the AUKUS partnership;

- "developing the ADF's ability to precisely strike targets at longer range and manufacture munitions in Australia;

- "improving the ADF's ability to operate from Australia's northern bases;

- lifting our capacity to rapidly translate disruptive new technologies into ADF capability, in close partnership with Australian industry;

- "investing in the growth and retention of a highly-skilled Defence workforce; and

- "deepening our diplomatic and defence partnerships with key partners in the Indo-Pacific."

The government needs as well to work closely with Indo-Pacific partners, notably in "the Pacific and Southeast Asia." This also requires a "stable relationship" with China. "Australia will continue to cooperate with China where we can, disagree where we must, manage our differences wisely, and, above all else, engage in and vigorously pursue our own national interest."

Nevertheless, the DSR was not accompanied by a companion piece in terms of an increase in defence spending that would reflect the document's emphasis on the near- and longer-term challenges by China in the here and now. As Ben Packham noted in a 9 May 2023 article on the budget: "But despite warnings of the need for an urgent transformation of the Australian Defence Force to meet unprecedented challenges, the Defence budget is forecast to remain steady for the next four years at about 2 per cent of GDP. Nominal Defence funding will rise by just under 7 per cent in the coming financial year, or about the rate of inflation. Vital new capabilities will take years to arrive. By June next year, only about $1.6bn is forecast to be spent on new guided weapons for the navy, out of a total $6.3bn program."[2]

The Defence Minister and Deputy Prime Minister Richard Marles in a speech given to News Corps' Defending Australia dinner in Canberra on 22 May 2023 put the DSR in the context of an overall balanced policy towards China. "So when the entirety of the story around China is examined, it is complex. Managing the relationship is difficult. It cannot be done on fundamentalist terms. We are stabilising the relationship with China, without compromising our national interest and our sovereignty. And in the process, we are being treated far more seriously as a country."[3]

The DSR and Australian Defence

But the review left much undecided and most commentators focused precisely on what the course of change would actually look like. And there is the problem of NOT increasing the defence budget precisely when with Taiwan crisis and the U.S. and Japanese response is to focus on readiness and ops tempo, accounts likely to be raided for the new programmatic initiatives.

The budget gap was a primary focus of the comments by Marcus Hellyer. As he underscored: "The Albanese government's May De-

---

2. https://www.theaustralian.com.au/nation/defence/billions-on
-the-table-but-its-slowly-as-she-goes/news-story/0f01dc3b2bf5b
550942a43e78f60a3de

3.
https://www.theaustralian.com.au/nation/defence/billions-on
-the-table-but-its-slowly-as-she-goes/news-story/0f01dc3b2bf5b
550942a43e78f60a3de

fence budget is disconnected from its own Defence Strategic Review. Defence funding and the plan for spending is business as usual when instead we need urgent action. Simply committing to the now seven-year-old budget line set by the former Coalition government in the 2016 Defence White Paper for the next four years is defence policy on autopilot. The budget papers show that the Defence Strategic Review is not yet integrated into Defence's budgets and plans. So compounding problems, competing priorities and challenges–like how AUKUS will be funded; the impact of the nuclear submarines on the rest of the budget, force structure and acquisition program; and the worsening failure to recruit and retain the numbers of military people to operate the force that's being built—have been left unresolved.

"To paraphrase Hegel, the heart of the problem in the 2023-24 Defence budget is a failure to start at the beginning: from a thesis setting out the defence force the country ideally needs to meet its strategic circumstances, then confronting it with an antithesis--the amount of money the government would prefer to spend on defence, and then synthesising these into an affordable but effective force structure somewhere in between."[4]

John Blackburn argued that what was needed was a national strategic review, not just a narrowly scoped ADF review. Blackburn argued: "The DSR also identifies that a central component of deterrence for national defence is resilience. It explains that critical requirements for a resilient nation include:

- an informed public,

- national unity and cohesion,

---

4. https://strategicanalysis.org/australias-defence-budget-is-living-in-the-past/

- democratic assuredness,

- robust cyber security, data networks and space capabilities,

- supply chain diversity,

- economic security,

- environmental security,

- fuel and energy security,

- enhanced military preparedness,

- advanced munitions manufacturing,

- robust national logistics, and

- a national industrial base with a capacity to scale.

"There is no indication from Government of how it intends to address these resilience components; listing them is not acting. In each case there needs to be a risk assessment before a strategy and plan can be developed. For example, given national concerns regarding the state of our energy systems and import dependencies, it is sobering to realise that the last time we had a National Energy Security Assessment, i.e., an energy risk assessment, was in 2011! *And the plan is?*"[5]

Stephen Frühling highlighted the gap between aspirations and commitments in the DSR. "Public discussion of the defence strategic review has focused on the announced changes to major capability

---

5. https://defence.info/defence-decisions/2023/05/the-missing-australian-national-security-strategy/

programs. On that score, the statement by Defence Minister Richard Marles that the DSR is 'the most ambitious review of Defence's posture and structure since the Second World War' is hard to reconcile with its recommendations, as there were few specific changes beyond those to Army which had been long expected. A few short paragraphs on the way that Australia should fundamentally change its approach to defence planning and force design, however, hint at very consequential change—and it is important that the government does not lose sight of their importance, despite them not receiving an explicit mention in the minister's statement."[6]

Greg Sheridan of *The Australian* noted after the DSR release: "Strategy without dollars is just noise. We should bear this undeniable reality in mind as we try to work out just what the Albanese government's Defence Strategic Review means for Australia."

As he then characterized the thinking underlying the review: "Take the dollars first. Australian defence is based on four simple propositions which together constitute a non-sequitur of madness. Proposition One: we face uniquely dangerous strategic circumstances. Proposition Two: the ADF is "not fit for purpose" in this environment. Proposition Three: we will not spend a single dollar more on defence than what has been planned for years and years. Proposition Four: we will make only marginal, incremental and very

---

6. https://www.aspistrategist.org.au/the-defence-strategic-review-a-revolution-in-australian-defence-planning/

slow changes to the ADF, and nothing of any real consequence in the five years ahead.[7]

In an additional piece, Sheridan underscored the only partial nature of the force structure review as highlighted in DSR: "One of the strangest decisions is to announce a new review – yes that's right, yet another review – into the shape of Australia's naval surface fleet. After countless billions of dollars and more reviews than hot meals, our navy has just three modern surface warships, the air warfare destroyers."[8]

At the outset and during months of waiting, the public was informed that they were going receive something akin to the Dibb review named for Paul Dibb and published in 1986. I think is safe to say that they didn't but worse is that because Paul Dibb is still very active, he could comment himself on the analogy, which he did in an article in *The Australian*.

"The point is that under the old policy regime, Australia was able to get away with a small peacetime defence force at peacetime levels of preparedness, capable of little more than routine peacetime operations and training, supported by an Australian Intelligence Community, policy community and industry base also at peacetime levels. Clearly this is no longer appropriate.

"Although the DSR says little on it, it is clear that readiness and sustainability are now a major concern. For example, the review says

---

7. https://www.theaustralian.com.au/inquirer/delays-defects-why
-we-are-sleepwalking-towards-a-defence-tragedy/news-story/9ea
061bdce138122134be6a73c360ca3

8. https://www.theaustralian.com.au/commentary/whats-the-poi
nt-of-the-dsr-if-we-need-yet-more-reviews/news-story/6ec5e7c3
c0ffc9438955df2c839f9550

in effect that a platform without crew or weapons is a waste of time and money.

"It makes explicit the need to increase aircrew numbers. This is a serious indictment of current Defence culture. The review does not provide an indication of the costs of fixing this problem but implies that they will prove significant. The review's support for the acquisition of uncrewed platforms (submarines and the RAAF's Ghost Bat autonomous air vehicle are mentioned) – and for a program for manufacturing modern and highly capable precision-guided weapons in Australia – is most welcome.

"This is for two reasons. It will enable Australia to move quickly to implement the policy of deterrence by denial, especially through long-range precision strike missiles. And it offers a more convincing mode for timely force expansion than the previous, largely implicit assumption that force expansion would be through the acquisition of additional, complex and costly major platforms. It is perhaps significant that the review does not propose the acquisition of further major platforms beyond those already planned, although the recommended independent analysis of the navy's surface fleet could well propose such changes."

The article concludes: "History provides a caution: only four years after the 1987 defence white paper, Defence was advising the then defence minister that should "financial allocations fall below no real growth over the decade, such a reduced program would preclude the maintenance of a strategy of defence in depth as outlined in the white paper". It is reassuring, then, that the Prime Minister, when launching the DSR, acknowledged that there would be a requirement for increased defence spending beyond the forward estimates. We must hope that he keeps his word."[9]

Finally, the former head of the Australian Strategic Policy Institute, Peter Jennings, warned that the DSR fails on the credibility dimension. He characterized the DSR as follows: "In the face of a rapidly deteriorating strategic outlook the government has squandered its best opportunity to make the case for a redesigned ADF. This is a patched-together baby of Frankenstein policy document, delivering no new money, a gaping wound in army, bucketloads of extra reviews and the delivery of vital equipment pushed years into the future."[10]

Let me conclude this chapter with an interview I did with Professor Blaxland in later March 2023 prior to the Williams Seminar and a month prior to the DSR release. This interview put the entire DSR effort into context.

Blaxland started by focusing on core questions which will be raised quickly in the public debate. "Whatever the recommendations, how will changes be resourced and implemented?" He warned that there could be a propensity to have an ongoing bureaucratic focus on the review, more interested in process and the broader question of rethink, than upon actually improving the capability for Australian defence.

Blaxland quoted the late Jim Molan to the point that Australia needed a broad national strategic review and policy within which a

---

9. https://www.theaustralian.com.au/inquirer/show-us-the-mone y-history-cautions-against-defence-spending-failure/news-story/ 7fb8f312f3c151ceb616dffbfde3522a

10. https://www.theaustralian.com.au/inquirer/frankensteinstyle -defence-strategic-review-fails-on-credibility/news-story/9b2cba c2f4a3daf1ebe69b99825c86fa

defence review would occur. A defence review is simply too narrow given the nature of the challenges posed by China to Australia.

In my own work, I have emphasized the importance of dealing with the Chinese approach to globalization which has put the liberal democracies in a subordinate position as a key part of any credible rethink of Pacific defence. Blaxland agreed with this point.

Blaxland underscored that the current government has rejected language used by the Morrison government as being too militaristic and too critical of China. Having avoided the question of why you are doing a defence review and focusing on what you need to do in the changed situation makes it difficult to have the kind of public narrative Australia will need to persuade the public and Australia's partners in the region.

So how will the delivery of the defence review be accompanied by a credible and effective public narrative?

With regard to shaping a credible and cohesive national narrative, Blaxland raised concerns with regard to the energy initiative of the government and the deal they cut with the Greens as one element of the context. The Greens are the most anti-military and anti-AUKUS political group of influence in Australian politics. What impact does this agreement on energy and Labor's elevating the importance of the Greens have on the broader defence debate, discussion and narrative? AUKUS will be embedded in the broader defence review, so that criticism which has already emerged within the Labor Party about AUKUS will be carried forward into the Strategic Defence Review itself.

Blaxland underscored that there is a clear need for more effective strategic messaging in an era of unrestricted competition or what some have called the weaponization of everything. That is sure why there is a need for a broader national strategy for Australia to compete effectively in a world of 21st century authoritarian conflict with the liberal democracies.

Blaxland described the period we have entered as being one of three intersecting circles of a Venn diagram. One circle might be labelled great power contestation; the second circle might be labelled looming environmental catastrophe; and the third might be labelled governance challenges in the liberal democracies.

How does AUKUS and the Strategic Defence Review fit into this world?

In short, the Defence Strategic Review is not the end of the discussion but simply a launch point for the discussion of what realistically is the way ahead for Australian defence, and a good part of answering that question will not even be about the ADF.

Chapter Nine

Shaping the Way Ahead

N o single Defence Strategic Review will be able to capture the sweep of how Australia will shape its way ahead in defence in the Indo-Pacific region. It can reorient but it cannot resolve the question of what the way ahead will actually be. This will depend on developments in the region and beyond, the actions of adversaries, allies, and partners, what they do, what they become, and what they will and will not do to Australia, with Australia, or against Australia.

It is a new historical epoch which Australia has entered along with the rest of the world, and debating the course of change for the ADF is occurring against the broader backdrop of a world in fundamental change.

And what has changed is the direct impact of the increased role of the twenty-first-century authoritarian powers enhancing their role in shaping the global order, along with significant change in the liberal democratic allies of Australia who share the same fate as Australia even when their paths are cross cutting. Australia can no longer rely on a single global partner to shape the path ahead in this global restructuring but faces the challenge of playing a much greater role of anchoring Indo-Pacific defence for the evolving democratic order in co-opetition with the authoritarian partners.

It is an island continent with a limited population, a significant agricultural and mining nation, cross-buffeted by significant global changes, with severe vulnerabilities due to the global trading system, and with the absence of significant manufacturing clout but yet providing a geography which can anchor the combined efforts of the democratic allies and partners in the Indo-Pacific region.

Any consideration of the way ahead for Australian defence proceeds within this changing global context and in the challenges to playing an anchoring role for the democracies seeking to deter Chinese aggression in the region and beyond. It is in this context that we need to consider some of the key factors in shaping a way ahead for Australian defence.

Each of the twelve factors highlighted in this chapter have been discussed at length with Australian officials, ADF officers, or Australian strategists. And each is rooted in these conversations with regard to the growing role which Australia plays and can play in the changing geographical context where the reach of digital, information warfare, and military systems has included Australia in the first line of Indo-Pacific defence.

Crafting a National Deterrence Doctrine

Precisely because the challenges from China are comprehensive, shaping only a strategy for the ADF misses the point. Whether considering trade, information war, cyber intrusion, or political and economic engagement within the domestic society, the Chinese reshaping of the global order is not narrowly military.

And with the dynamics of change in the United States and Britain, no amount of AUKUS will solve the challenge for Australia to shape a national resilience and security strategy.[1]

An April 2023 discussion with Dr. Andrew Carr of Australian National University focused on the challenge to Australian political culture of actually crafting a national deterrent doctrine and strategy. Carr underscored: "What are we deterring China from doing? This is not just a military task. We need to address it publicly, both to gain ongoing support from the public but also to clarify what we expect from government coordination across the whole of government to deter China.

"Deterrence is very new in the Australian experience. We have been part of a Western coalition for a very long time, but we have never had to do the kind of messaging and communication which is a crucial part of deterrence. There is not a lot of muscle memory in Australia for deterrent discourse."

China has become a different kind of competitor and adversary and partner as it changed from the reform years and building its economy to that of the China under President Xi who is combining elements of power to shape the global system more in the Chinese image.

What will Australia accept in working with its main trade partners? And what will it not? What role will foreign students from China play in Australian universities? What actions by China are clearly to be countered? Which tolerated? Which ignored?

All of this is part of shaping deterrent language and narrative. What tools does Australia need to deter against which types of actions? Where does the military fit into a broader deterrent effort? Such an

---

1. See the work on resilience done by the Integrated Economic Research–Australia. https://www.jbcs.co/iieraustralia-about

effort involves the broader Australia economic, social, cultural, information and security interests and not just limited to professional military competence.

Carr's key point is that such questions need to be central to Australian debate and consideration, and regularly so. There are ongoing considerations of what is to be deterred and what means need to be developed to do so.

Carr concluded our conversation by highlighting a central problem facing Western policy makers. Simply put, with the end of the Cold War and the seeming end of history and the victory of liberal democracy underwritten by the United States, policy makers saw the rules-based order as global with little clarity with regard to what are core versus peripheral interests. The term global commons came into vogue and suggested a global interdependent order in which interests were dictated by the need to deal with the gaps in the seams wherever and whenever they occurred.

Deterrence is national in character and to be effective requires clarity with regard to core interests versus peripheral interests. It also requires a realistic sense of limits. What can the nation actually do that will be seen as credible by the adversary? And will the nation have the will to do so?

As Carr put it: "The grey zone challenge comes from this global lack of clarity. With our "rules-based order" language, we tend to suggest that everything in the status quo is of interest for the West. Chinese actions in the South China Sea and Russia's actions in Crimea in 2014, called our bluff.

"Deterrence is then a policy of limits as well as focus. But it cannot remain a policy only pursued by the military, while absent from the discussions of the political class and the public."

China's relationship with Australia shaped in the past two decades cannot continue; but what kind of relationship can it be? What are its limits and what are the paths of cooperation and the focus of deterrence?

The Art of Statecraft and Crisis Management

A key capability flows from shaping an ability to craft, execute, revise, and navigate a national deterrent doctrine, namely the art of statecraft. The art of statecraft is a largely missing ingredient in Western military policy for a long time—the military in the past two decades is dispatched somewhere and comes home after largely inconclusive or negative strategic results. AUKUS certainly cannot help with this because the United States and the United Kingdom have been practitioners of the dispatch and send force practice without much correlation with strategic gain or result.

The Defence Strategic Review does underscore the importance of the art of statecraft in the way ahead for Australian defence strategy. As noted, "Statecraft must be driven and directed by a clear sense of national strategy and be coordinated across government through a clear and holistic national strategic approach. Defence's role in this whole-of-nation strategy is critical. Military power enables pursuit of a wide range of Australian interests in peacetime and is fundamental to deterring conflict, defending Australia, and denying an adversary in the event of armed conflict."[2]

But as the late Brendan Sargeant discussed with me, the Australian government faced major challenges in shaping an effective way ahead

---

2. National Defence Strategic Review, Australian Government, 2023 p. 30.

to add the kind of capabilities necessary to exercise the art of statecraft using military forces. In a meeting in 2019, we discussed this challenge at some length. As he noted at the outset of our conversation: "Globalization has unleashed one set of forces; the rise of nationalism another set of forces; and the rise of the illiberal powers yet a different set of force. Nations are trying to work out how best to protect their interests and with whom to work to do so."

This has a significant impact on the inherited alliances. There is the habitual cooperation which has underlaid the Western Alliances and that cooperation is continuing but in the context of a significant redefinition of what alliances are going to look like going forward. "Great powers like the United States are more interested in totalizing alliance arrangements than their alliance partners are likely to accept. Australians like other regional allies of the United States will seek working arrangements with a variety of regional partners to provide for our interests and work through different sorts of working arrangements to deal with our strategic challenges."

The shift is clearly from followership to engagement in working relationships where leadership is shouldered or shared differently from the great power followership role which Australia has followed first with Britain and then with the United States. Working relationships with regional or global partners around specific issues and challenges are becoming the "real" alliances. They are being built in response to specific crisis or specific problems.

For Australia, the challenge will be how to deal with global and regional crisis management. For defence, this means shaping capability which can be leveraged in a crisis and effectively used by political leadership effectively to meet the national interest. This means taking a hard look at the kind of defence force which Australia has and is developing and determining which tools are available to decision makers. It also means building a more durable and sustainable force through a crisis period.

"The ability to deploy force creates more decision space in a crisis. But you need to do that over time. That requires a robust logistical and industrial base that can give you more confidence that you can scale up during a crisis." From a policy perspective, you want to give yourself more strategic options by giving yourself more time. Which means that you will need to have a more sustainable force during a crisis."

And the crisis management challenge requires thinking through partnerships and working relationships with allies. "When do you exercise leadership? When do you exercise followership?"

An example of how force packaging might be reworked in terms of partnerships in the region could be the working relationship between Australia and Indonesia. "We ought to be able to put together an integrated task force with Indonesia to manage a regional crisis from the low end to the high end. And a task force where either Australia or Indonesia could take the lead."

In short, according to Sargeant, "We need to think differently about our position in this part of the world and how that may drive our thinking about the capability which we need to have and to develop going forward."

Working the Geography

Let me turn again to the question of geography within the rework of Australian defence. There are a number of different aspects of the geographical dimension of shaping a way ahead for Australian defence strategy. First, there is the question of how to leverage the geography of Australia to enhance national defence viability and survivability.

Second, there is the question of how Australia can provide innovative new ways to support allies lacking geographical depth in the region. Third, there is the question of where ADF forces need to operate within the Indo-Pacific region to provide effective crisis management and deterrence effects. And, finally, there is the crucial question of how Australia works its neighbourhood effectively as an incubator against Chinese intrusions.

Here I will primarily deal briefly with the first two aspects of the geography dimension.

Leveraging Australia's geography is a key part of shaping an effective way ahead for the direct defence of Australia. Australia's geography can play a key role, in both providing for deployment and sustainment mobility as well as providing diverse launch points for longer range effects, alone or with allied engagement from Australian territory.

Again, I turned to Dr. Andrew Carr for a discussion of this aspect of shaping a way ahead for Australian defence strategy. Carr reminded me that the question of the use of territory in the direct defence of Australia has a long history. "Looking back at Australian history, there has been experience which can be drawn on as we look forward. And much of our investment in the ADF has focused on infrastructure in Australia. But with the more direct challenge posed by China, there is a re-think and re-focus going on with regard to how best to leverage Australian territory in our defence posture."

The focus now is upon "what are the key areas of Australia for defence efforts, whether population centers, bases, supply centers, production centers and so on. In effect, what is being considered is an archipelago concept in terms of understanding how the Australian territorial chessboard can be most effectively utilized in deterrence and defence."

This has an important impact on the Australian Army, for example, as the Army shifts from a primary focus on being an expeditionary force going somewhere globally, to being a key enabler of the direct defence of Australia and leveraging Australian territory as an enabler in regional defence and deterrence. The Northern and Western parts of Australia provide significant territory in such an effort, but resources and population are scarce to do so. But new technologies—notably various autonomous technologies, such as UAVs, USVs, UUVs, and ground robotic vehicles—provide for new ways to leverage Australian territory even in the presence of limited civilian infrastructure.

If one thinks of Australian territory as a launchpad for operations into the region, then how do you organise the ADF to do so? How do you work with core allies such as the United States and Japan to share use of territory for projection of force? What kind of new basing solutions might be created to share operations between Australians and allies and to enable more robust ADF national operations?

Care noted: "We are perhaps talking about a new alliance bargain for Australia. We would work together as coalition partners, and we would be doing tasks towards a common mission.

"But I think clarity about how Australia contributes to the alliance, what Australia is getting from that alliance are actually going to be first order questions in order to make the specific operations from Australian soil more effective.

"If we just simply have more Japanese forces and more American forces here on Australian soil, and they're replicating what the Australians are trying to do, or they're competing for use of the key locations and key airfields, and things like that, then there's going to be real challenges and impediments to operations and potentially negative public spillover from such strategic confusion."

Carr concluded: "When we think in terms of a chessboard or archipelagic metaphor, then some of the distinctions between what is specifically Australian territory and what kind of forward presence points are crucial will start to become clearer. It will be our ability to move between a whole range of access points that will be absolutely critical."

Operating Within and From Australian Territory

Re-configuring the ADF to operate across Australian geography for survivability will be a major challenge, which will take time, imagination, and money. Operating in more austere areas also raises the question of the location of manpower and the challenge of being able to move critical resources such as fuel and weapons to austere locations within Australia.

As Air Vice-Marshal Michael Kitcher, Deputy Chief Joint Operations (DCJOPS), underscored in my interview with him in April 2023: "The really good thing about Australia is the size of Australia and the amount of nothing that is in Australia. The really bad thing about Australia is the size of Australia and the amount of nothing that is in Australia."

Australia's population and economic base is in the south and east of the country; the core defence locations for projecting force into the region are in the north, north east, and north west of Australia. Northern Australia (especially the north and north west) is lightly populated without significant infrastructure and major industrial base. How does Australia have capabilities which can be used to project force into the region from Northern Australia, but the majority of the population and industrial base remains well in the south?

For example, the RAAF has a number of bare bases in northern Australia in addition to their main operating bases. But how can those bases really be used for operations in a crisis, and flexibly use all of the basing options available? How to support all these locations? How to move fuel and weapons? How to ensure the necessary level of resilience and that combat support, logistics, and health elements are available? There are no easy or cheap solutions to achieving a viable outcome.

Air Vice-Marshal Kitcher concluded: "The challenge of how we optimize the Australian geography for defence is real and is quite significant. As is how we use Australian geography for the best effect of allies and partners that we might invite to deploy here. This is an ongoing process and a real challenge."

In an additional interview in April 2023, Air Vice-Marshal Darren Goldie, the air commander of the RAAF, provided further insight into this challenge from the operator's point of view. Our engagement through two decades in the Middle East has arguably driven us down a single service route to force generation, focused on expeditionary operations, hosted from secure bases. We now need to look to evolve our approach to joint force generation from Australian territory. We don't have the level of knowledge and normative experience we need to generate regarding infrastructure across Western and Northern Australia for the Australian version of agile combat employment."

He contrasted the Australian to the PACAF approach to agility. The USAF in his view was working on how to trim down support staff for air operations and learning how to use multiple bases in the Pacific, some of which they owned and some of which they did not own. In contrast, the Australian concept he was highlighting was focused on Australian geography and how the joint force and the infrastructure which could be built—much of it mobile—could allow for dispersed air combat operations. This meant in his view that "we need to have a clear understanding of the fail and no-fail enablers" for the kind of dispersed operations necessary to enhance the ADF's deterrent capability.

A key element of this is C2. Rather than looking to traditional CAOC battle management, the focus needs as well to be on C2 in a dispersed or disaggregate way, where the commander knows what is available to them in an area of operations and aggregate those forces into an integrated combat element operating as a distributed entity. Goldie commented: "We are developing concepts about how we will do command and control on a more geographic basis. This builds on our history with Darwin and Tindal to a certain extent, although technology has widened that scale to be a truly continental distributed control concept. We already are familiar with how an air asset like the Wedgetail can take over the C2 of an air battle when communications are cut to the CAOC, but we don't have a great understanding of how that works from a geographic basing perspective. What authorities to move aircraft, people and other assets are vested in local area Commanders that would be resilient to degradation in communications from the theatre commander—or JFACC? We need to focus on how we can design our force to manoeuvre effectively using our own territory as the chessboard."

Air Vice-Marshal Goldie underscored that the ability to work with limited resources to generate air combat capability is exercised regularly by the normal activity of 75 Squadron, flying F-35s in Australia's Air Combat Group. This squadron operates from RAAF Base Tindal in the Northern Territory and as Goldie put it: "they have to operate with what they have in a very austere area."

By learning how to use Australian territory to support agile air operations, and to take those capabilities to partner or allied operational areas, Australia will significantly enhance its deterrent capabilities going forward.

Force Distribution and Integration

In my book with Ed Timperlake on the building of the kill-web ecosystem for concepts of operations and force development, this is how we described force distribution and integration in shaping a way ahead for force development: "Force packages or combat clusters are deployed under mission command with enough organic C2 and ISR to monitor their situations and integrate the platforms that are part of that combat cluster and to operate effectively at a point of interest. Within that combat cluster, the C2 and ISR systems allow for reachback to non-organic combat assets which are then conjoined operational for a period of time to that combat cluster and becomes part of an expanded modular task force.

"Such an approach and capabilities are the essence of what a kill-web enabled force is and how such integratability can close the geographical and combat seams which twenty-first-century authoritarian powers are focused on generating. This allows for the kind of escalation management and control crucial for the competition with the twenty-first-century authoritarian powers.

"It is not about getting to World War III as rapidly as possible or generating nuclear exchanges early in a widening conflict. It is about escalation control and management, and an ability to close seams which adversaries seek to open to gain significant escalation dominance as they expand the reach and range of those twenty-first-century authoritarian powers.

"A shift to a kill web approach with regard to force development, training and operations is a foundation from which the U.S. and its allies can best leverage the force we have and the upgrade paths to follow. For this approach to work, there is a clear need for a different kind of C2 and ISR infrastructure to enable the shift in concepts of operations . . .

"A very different kind of C2 and ISR infrastructure is at hand to build enablement for distributed operations. The new C2 and ISR infrastructure requires rethinking considerably the nature of decision making and the viability of the classic notion of the Observe, Orient, Decide and Act (OODA) loop. If the machines are fusing data or doing the OO function, then the DA part of the equation becomes transformed, notably if done in terms of decision making at the tactical edge. The decisions at the edge will drive a reshaping of the information about the battlespace because actors at the tactical edge are recreating the information environment itself."[3]

The United States and the ADF are on convergent paths with regard to such developments, sharing technology, C2/ISR arrangements, and a number of key elements to shape a distributed force operationally with integrated combat effects. The level of collaboration between the United States and the ADF is historically unprecedented and opens up the possibility of scalability in terms of the operations of the two forces. Although the two allied militaries closely collaborate, they represent different nations with overlapping but different interests. Force distribution will focus on the survival of the national

---

3. Robbin F Laird and Edward Timperlake, A Maritime Kill Web Force in the Making: Deterrence and Warfighting in the 21st Century (pp. 41-43). Kindle Edition.

forces but with an ability to work with the other nation in providing for strategic depth for the other.

For the ADF, force distribution starts with leveraging the national territory and being able to have a resilient force supported from national territory. It proceeds out into the neighbourhood with the ability of the combined air and naval force to project power out to Australia's first island chain with the Army able to move rapidly forces to reinforce partners in the region when facing pressures in the region.

This gets back to the geography factor mentioned earlier, namely where ADF forces need to operate within the Indo-Pacific region to provide effective crisis management and deterrence effects. The ADF is a modest force, well trained in coalition operations, but the direct defence of Australia even with expanded reach means that the ADF's core capability needs to be able to operate from the Australian "sanctuary" outwards to the first island chain, and when necessary for deterrent effect or crisis management, to operate beyond the first island chain.

Where does the ADF primarily need to operate? With what kind of joint force? With which allies and partners? And with what capabilities?

The shift from the wars of choice in the Middle East to the defence of Australia within its region is a major one which clearly will affect force structure development. As Air Vice-Marshal Michael Kitcher, Deputy Chief Joint Operations (DCJOPS), put it in my April 2023 interview with him: "The focus in this period, up to say 2017, for CJOPS was on operations in the Middle East whilst managing operations in our region. We clearly have leveraged the earlier experiences in our renewed focus on the conduct of Operations, Actions and Activities (OAA) in the Indo-Pacific. We are focused on developing a theatre campaign plan to translate strategic guidance into the OAA we execute in our region to achieve our desired objectives.

"We are focused on ways we can operate as a joint force to optimise our regional OAA to have the maximum positive effect in supporting our theater campaign plan. You don't get the maximum benefits from a joint force unless firstly the services provide you with trained personnel capable of executing joint missions and then HQJOC, through focused joint planning, maximises the potential of the individual components. We have made good progress along this path but still have a way to go."

Air Vice-Marshal Kitcher highlighted that we are "now squarely focused on managing operations in a coordinated fashion in our region." And this means both, how to get the best joint force effect but also how to coordinate the ADF effort with core allies in also getting the best proper coalition effect.

Obviously in working with coalition partners, national sovereignty has to be respected but at the same time for effectiveness in operations, coalition forces need to operate in an integrated manner. This is a key tension which needs to be managed; notably in crises where the government of the day will make decisions about the allowable operations of their national forces, these individual decisions may challenge the effectiveness of a coalition force.

This is a challenge which CJOPS has to be prepared to deal with in both exercises and real-world operations. Kitcher underscored: "Planning and exercises prepare the way for joint and coalition capabilities but executing them in an actual operational situation requires agility and flexibility of command by CJOPS and his staff, and our parallel staff in the various coalition headquarters."

Air Vice-Marshal Kitcher emphasised that working with partners to deal with challenges in the region has clearly grown in importance for both deterrent and operational impacts. The relationship with US forces has certainly become closer. He mentioned an upcoming CPX exercise with the US Indo-PACOM command in which the ADF and the United States will run a detailed CPX on a regional scenario together. The cooperation with both Japan and India is also growing.

And with Australia's regional defence emphasis, joint operations will need to focus on regional partners in the Australian neighbourhood. This will see more emphasis on building regional expertise and continued engagement with regional countries through relationship building, languages, cultural awareness, and local knowledge. This can provide an important aspect of Australian leadership in a regional military coalition but dependent on the crisis, a differentiator for Australian involvement as well.

As Air Vice-Marshal Kitcher summarised their job: "We've got a responsibility to make sure that we optimize how well the joint force works together for the greatest positive effect and present the best possible options to government on how that force might be employed. We've also got a remit to ensure that we can work as closely and as efficiently and effectively as possible with our regional partners in both peacetime HADR situations and potential crisis situations.

"We've got a responsibility to be as efficient and as effective together among like-minded nations' militaries. If we are not careful, uncoordinated actions in our region will overwhelm smaller countries and not have a positive effect. Planning and conducting OAA together ensures we present a much more credible regional security capability than we do as individual nations. "The militaries have a large part of the responsibility to generate how we can do so. And then it's up to individual governments to determine how those forces will be employed at any one time or in any one set of security circumstances."

Kitcher mentioned the role of training and exercises which are becoming crucial in determining the way ahead not just operationally but in terms of force structure development as well. In my earlier discussion with Conway, he underscored the central role which advanced training plays in shaping the kind of force structure development which can manage the "triangle of tradeoffs."

As he put it: "Within a limited budget, you've now got to think really, really hard about survivability. And you've got to think really hard about preparedness and that links to the training piece which is increasingly important. One way of mitigating that risk is getting your training systems right. And being able to fight the best fight with what you've got and invest in warfare rather than just war fighting."

Force Distribution, Sustainment, and Logistical Support

To ensure enhanced survivability, the ADF is looking to distribute over Australian territory more effectively. But this makes logistical support for distributed forces a major strategic challenge. And with the changing threat calculus, the force needs to have greater endurance which requires enhanced sustainability.

So the question is, how best to combine distribution of combat forces, with effective logistical support, but have credible sources of supply that can sustain the force?

In many ways, this poses a significant strategic triangle — force mobility, sustainability, and logistics — which has to be built and operated in the period ahead to have an effective ADF and, of course, the ADF is not alone in terms of meeting this challenge. Most notably, its major warfighting ally in the Pacific, the United States, faces the tyranny of the Pacific in dealing with this strategic matrix.

I have discussed this challenge with Colonel David Beaumont of the Australian Army several times in the past few years as he has worked on logistics issues his entire service life. Currently, he is the director of Joint Professional Military Education at the Australian Defence College located in Canberra. As Beaumont characterised the challenge in our latest discussion in April 2023: "Sustainment and logistics capabilities determine the endurance of your force. They shape the ability of your force to remain operable. They determine how your force can sequence its operations and operate at the tip of the spear. It can be described as the arbiter of opportunity to paraphrase Thomas Kane. By that I mean, it determines when the force can and cannot act."

We are experiencing a major shift from just-in-time wars and just-in-time delivery systems to facing the challenge of response to crises created by adversaries which will challenge our ability to act, endure, and prevail. As Beaumont put it: "We have been used to certain ways of operating in the past 20 years or so. We have operated in surges and cycles that have been well planned in advance and shaped our routines. Forces have been allocated on the basis of what we can reasonably sustain. For a country like Australia, we have been able to choose judiciously the forces we can operate with because we know we can sustain them at the right moment and with the right resources."

The challenge now is to prepare for a different scale and intensity of conflict which simply does not comply with limited sustainability and just-in-time logistics. Beaumont added: "We will need now to operate at the maximum of our potential and that requires logistics resources and sustainability planning to suit."

We turned to the real challenge of getting procurement systems in Australia or the United States to be able to prioritise sustainment and logistics as a strategic issue rather than a residual one. Beaumont argued that Western military acquisition systems have for a long time prioritised platform acquisition over operational sustainability and preparedness, with corporate success often defined by the perceived effectiveness of platform delivery programs. This emphasis means that moneys tend to be drawn from sustainment or logistics budgets to pay for new platforms or cost over runs of platform programs.

How then does one change this culture and focus?

Beaumont noted that one way to do so that is being started in Australia is to deal with specific commodities capability needs to be dealt with as a program in its own right, such as the newly launched guided weapons program. It is also important to go beyond headline logistics deficiencies and resolving broader sustainment gaps across the force.

When one considers the problem of mobilisation of resources from the general economy, it is easier to conceptualise rather than do or fund. If Australia wishes to pursue greater self-reliance in stocks, then mobilisation is an inevitable subject which needs to become real in terms of programs and funding.

There is the question of enhancing production with allies in order to have an allied-wide approach to production in a new arsenal of democracy model. But the challenge remains for each of the countries involved in joint production or acquisition of stocks available in times of crisis to the national forces.

Then there is the question of logistical means to move stocks to forces which themselves are working the art of force mobility. The earlier discussed interview with the Air Commander Australia highlighted his concern with an enhanced ability for air mobility from diverse locations in Australia. But how to move the parts and supplies necessary to support such an agile operating RAAF?

And with a large territory, how will Australia produce, stockpile, and move the supplies necessary for itself and the allies who are using the Australian territory? This requires an effective national and allied interoperable IT system for logistics enterprise management as well as the ability to use maritime, rail, or road systems to move supplies to the point of need.

Force mobility, sustainability, and logistics have become a strategic triangle shaping the capability for force endurance, effectiveness, and relevance to conflict with the authoritarian powers in the twenty-first century.

Acquisition and Force Development

Along with the strategic shift towards distributed forces and operations prioritised in their neighbourhood, the build out of the ADF in the years ahead needs to be part of the great software evolution underway, and the expanded role of autonomous systems for the operating forces.

One example of the change is occurring in the domain of maritime autonomous systems. The nature of this change was highlighted in an interview which I did in April 2023 which followed up on the 2022 interview cited earlier with Commodore Darron Kavanagh, Director General Warfare Innovation, Royal Australian Navy Headquarters.

Maritime autonomous systems don't fit into the classic platform development mode or the sharp distinction between how particular platforms operate or perform and the various payloads they can carry. They are defined by the controlling software and the payloads they can deliver individually or as a wolfpack with the role of platforms subordinated to the effects they can deliver through their payloads. The software enables the payloads to be leveraged either individually, though more likely in combination as a wolfpack or a contributor to a combat cluster.

We started our discussion by focusing on mission threads as a way to understand the role and contribution of maritime autonomous systems. What missions does a combat commander need to accomplish? And how can maritime autonomous systems contribute to a mission thread for that combat commander, within the context of combat clusters?

As Commodore Kavanagh underscored: "One of the issues about how we've been looking at these systems is that we think in terms of using traditional approaches of capability realization with them. We are not creating a defence capability from scratch. These things exist, already, to a degree out in the commercial world, regardless of what defence does. AI built into robotic and autonomous systems are in the real world regardless of what the defence entities think or do. And we have shown through various autonomous warrior exercises, that we can already make important contributions to mission threads which combat commander's need to build out now and even more so going forward."

And that is really the next point. The use of maritime autonomous systems is driven by evolving concepts of operations and the mission threads within those evolving CONOPS rather than by a platform-centric traditional model of acquisition. Commodore Kavanagh pointed out that traditional acquisition is primarily focused on platform replacement and has difficulty in supporting evolving concepts of operations.

This is how he put it: "We're good at replacing platforms. That doesn't actually require a detailed CONOPS when we are just replacing something. But we now need to examine on a regular basis what other options do we have? How could we do a mission in a different way which would require a different profile completely?"

Put another way, combatant commanders can conduct mission rehearsals with their forces and can identify gaps to be closed. But the traditional acquisition approach is not optimised for closing such gaps at speed through the use of disruptive technologies. The deployment and development of autonomous systems are part of the response to the question of how gaps can be closed or narrowed rapidly and without expensive solution sets.

In an interview I did earlier this year with a senior U.S. Navy commander, he identified the "gaps" problem. "Rehearsal of operations sheds light on our gaps. if you are rehearsing, you are writing mission orders down to the trigger puller, and the trigger puller will get these orders and go, I don't know what you want me to do. Where do you want me to be? Who am I supposed to check in with? What do you want me to kill when I get there? What are my left and right limits? Do I have target engagement authority?

"This then allows a better process of writing effective mission orders so that we're actually telling the joint force what we want them to do and who's got the lead at a specific operational point. By such an approach, we are learning. We're driving requirements from the people who are actually out there trying to execute the mission, as opposed to the war gamers who were sitting on the staff trying to figure out what the trigger pullers should do."

But how to close the gaps?

As Commodore Kavanagh argued: "We need to deliver lethality at the speed of relevance. But if I go after the conventional solution, and I'm just replacing something, that's actually not a good use of my very finite resources. We need to be answering the operational commander's request to fill a gap in capability, even if it is a 30% solution compared to no solution on offer from the traditional acquisition process."

These are not technologies looked at in terms of a traditional acquisition process which requires them to go through a long period of development to form a platform which can be procured with a long-life use expectancy. Commodore Kavanagh simply pointed out that maritime autonomous systems are NOT technologies to be understood in this manner. "We build our platforms in a classical waterfall approach where you design, develop and build a platform over twenty years to make them excellent. But their ability to adapt quickly is very limited. This is where software intensive systems such as maritime autonomous systems are a useful complement to the conventional platforms. Maritime autonomous systems are built around software first approaches, and we are able to do rapid readjustments of the code in a combat situation."

And the legacy acquisition approach is not well aligned with the evolution of warfare. Not only is the focus changing to what distributed combat clusters can combine to do in terms of combat effects, but the payload impacts at a point of relevance is also becoming of increased salience to warfighting approaches.

What is emerging clearly is a need to adapt more rapidly than what traditional platforms and their upgrade processes can do. Gaps will emerge and need to be closed not just in mission rehearsals but in the combat operations to be anticipated in the current and future combat situations.

And to endure in conflict, it will be crucial as well to protect one's core combat capital capabilities and platforms which calls for increased reliance on capabilities like maritime autonomous systems to take the brunt of attrition in combat situations as capital ships become mother ships rather than simply being the core assets doing the brunt of combat with whatever organic capabilities they have onboard.

As Commodore Kavanagh noted: "The nuclear-powered submarine is absolutely necessary for what we need to do for our defence in depth, but what we're focused on with maritime autonomous systems completely complements it, because what I want to do is ensure that the dangerous stuff gets done by the autonomous forces as much as possible, because we can rebuild that capability much more rapidly. We can actually restore it whereas we can't restore a nuclear-powered submarine quickly if lost."

Commodore Kavanagh closed our discussion by emphasising the crucial need for Australia to have an ability to stay in the fight in case of conflict in the Pacific. He argued that having their own abilities to innovate in autonomous systems areas was part of such a desired capability.

"Resilience in a combat situation is an ability to be able to experiment and adjust on the fly. To have an enduring force that can operate until statecraft can shape an end state, the warriors and their support community must adjust the combat force rapidly to the real-world combat conditions. By shaping a deployment and ongoing development process in the maritime autonomous systems area, we are contributing to such a combat capability."[4]

Another take on the change in acquisition and the dynamics of change was highlighted at the Williams Foundation seminar held on 28 September 2022. At that seminar, the head of Force Design in the Australian Department of Defence, Major General Anthony Rawlins,

---

4. https://sldinfo.com/2023/05/the-role-of-maritime-autonomou s-systems-mission-thread-capabilities-to-meet-the-needs-of-mod ern-warfare/

addressed directly the question of how the ADF could realistically and effectively ramp up its capabilities in the midterm. This is how he put it: "Has the hardening of expensive, exquisite, arguably irreplaceable platforms now reached its logical zenith? This is manifest in the arguments for the cheap or the expendable as a supplement or potentially a replacement for expensive crewed platforms going forward.

"Defence is not just investing in exponential developments in autonomy, artificial intelligence, remote sensing, etc. as an R and D line of effort. But defence is doing so with a view to fielding capability in the immediate short term. And it hardly meets the definition of survivability to be investing in platforms and capabilities that are designed to be expendable."

And at the Williams Foundation Seminar on Next Generation Autonomous Systems, on April 8, 2021, Professor Jason Scholz, CEO of the Trusted Autonomous Systems Defence Cooperation Centre, put the challenge and opportunity for the ADF along similar lines. Here is what he emphasised during his presentation at the seminar: "Autonomous systems for air, land, sea, space, cyber, electromagnetic, and information environments offers huge potential to enhance Australia's critical and scarce manned platforms and soldiers, and realizing this now and into the future requires leadership in defence, in industry, in science and technology and academia with an ambition and an appetite for risk in effecting high-impact and disruptive change."

Scholz sees autonomous systems as providing mass to the distributed force. This is what he noted in my interview with him conducted after his seminar presentation: "Humans express mission command goals to machines, machines express to the operator what actions they can take to achieve that, and a contract agreement is formed. Within the commander's intent, machines then subcontract to other machines and so on, dynamically adapting as the battle evolves to build that Mosaic." In both his presentation and our interview after his presentation, he highlighted a capability on which they are working now that can provide for sensors and communications capabilities to support the force which complements manned assets to provide for Information, Reconnaissance, and Intelligence. In other words, autonomous systems can provide for sensor networks, which can be part of the effort to leverage information systems to deliver more timely and effective decisions.

The ADF is already undergoing a transition to shape a distributed integrated force. Next Generation Autonomous Systems can provide a further set of capabilities for a more effective, dense, survivable, and capable ADF as it builds out for operations in the Indo-Pacific region and enhances its defence of the Australian continent.

How software-driven payload to mission systems can accelerate ADF capabilities in the near to midterm was already highlighted in the work conducted earlier by the Plan Jericho team in their focus on the importance of being able to gain transient software advantage in conflict with adversaries. Where we are headed is in a direction which could yield significant operational advantages whereby code re-writing is driven by operations and operations by training, and training driving development and looping back again into operations.

The coming of autonomous systems is part of the software-first rapid redesign effort which will be a required feature of the way ahead for acquisition. Another is to leverage experience already gained in the past in rapid acquisition for special forces, and, in this sense, the forces need not just to be special but become a norm in terms of acquisition practice.

In a series I commissioned from Scott Graham Lovell in 2020, I asked him to take a wide view of the ADF and how to prepare them and Australia for an enduring conflict. In the piece which I published on 24 April, 2020, Lovel dealt with the agility challenge facing procurement.

This is what he argued: "The ever-changing face of the modern battlespace dictates that no defence force anywhere can possibly be prepared for all scenarios they might face on the battlefield. The modern enemy adapts quickly to emerging technology and tactics, and if we are to remain inside their OODA loop and retain battlefield superiority, we must also be able to adapt and react quickly. A big part of this agility for a modern Defence Force is its ability to assess issues and develop solutions in quick time, usually requiring Defence to procure capability enhancing materiel and get it in the hands of the warfighters ASAP.

"For the ADF, in reality this is done very well in some cases and very poorly in others. This article takes a look at the different types of ADF procurement, some examples of where this has been done well and not so well in meeting the immediate need of the warfighter, who does this the best in the ADF and some things that need to change in order for capability enhancement through material procurement to be done efficiently and effectively across the board."

In the article, he identified one part of the ADF that "gets it right" from an agility in procurement point of view. "There is at least one group in the ADF who know how to work the procurement model right. One group who always gets what they need, when they need it and it is not because the rules are different for this group, nor are they treated any differently in procurement circles . . . it is because they are competent, educated, agile and know how to get things done. I am speaking of the SOCOMD group (especially the SAS).

"What is so different about SOCOMD that ensures they always get what they need? They have a high operational priority—any requests out of this group is actioned without delay; they have an ample and flexible budget—no penny pinching when it comes to SOCOMD; they do one-off and unique procurements regularly—they have a clear and identified process for getting what they need; there is a clear and un-convoluted chain of command—approvals happen quickly with low level delegation limits understood; they have dedicated procurement support—they have their own CASG procurements team, Design Acceptance Representative (DAR), Log Support Chain, etc.; a pragmatic and efficient DAR—gets equipment approved for use by any means necessary; all personnel are trained and competent in the procurement and requisition process—they all know how to request what they need, develop the justification and business case, speed it through approval channels, etc.

"The wider ADF (including CASG staff) could all learn a thing or two about how SOCOMD goes about procurement."[5]

The Arsenal of Democracy: The Role of Australian Defence Industry

For Australia to have an enduring force and resilience through a crisis requires having supplies on hand or that which can be generated at home during that crisis. For this to happen, two key changes will have to occur.

The first is for the Australian defence industry to be expanded and the kind of ecosystem put in place within the economy and society to endure through a crisis period. This will take manpower, technology, manufacturing capability, and money.

---

5. https://defence.info/re-shaping-defence-security/2020/04/equipment-procurement-and-capability-the-agility-challenge/

The second is for the democratic partners of Australia to work much more closely together to shape an interactive arsenal of democracy. The blunt fact is that Australia cannot act as if the United States is the arsenal of democracy. The United States has reduced its defence industrial base dramatically over the years, as well as its industrial base. Australia is simply not an industrial country. One cannot assume that mobilisation of supply will be a simple switch-turning exercise. In today's world, it has to be built and funded. This is not an easy task nor one that is politically popular as well.

The Australian Department of Defence has favoured Foreign Military Sales arrangements with the United States. This has provided the ADF with proven products at a predictable cost but with overseas suppliers as essential providers of the just-in-time parts.

But a crisis in the Pacific will make such a strategy as one which will make the ADF a one-month duration military. The need is for a mix of Australian-supplied and stockpiled parts to be available to allow the ADF to operate at the level needed during a crisis.

The shortfalls evident during the current Ukraine War make it clear that simply depending on the United States as a supplier is inadequate even without the problems of transport in a crisis or the US military getting priority in a crisis. As Doug Cameron noted in a 21 May 2023, *Wall Street Journal* article: "The war in Ukraine has exposed myriad deficiencies in the U.S. defence industrial base's ability to surge weapons production. The brittle supply chain for computer chips has hobbled missile production, while the U.S. has struggled to produce enough 155 mm artillery shells for the Ukrainian army to fire at Russian forces.

"The U.S. has insufficient capacity to produce all of the materials that make things go bang, so-called energetics, which include explosives, the propellants that fire shells and bullets, and pyrotechnics for flares. The U.S. military relies on a single factory in Louisiana to produce black powder, an old-fashioned type of gunpowder that has hundreds of defence applications."[6]

Frankly, the most credible way ahead is for the United States, Australia, and close allies to shape an acquisition strategy which prioritises standardisation of items such as munitions and build them across a global geopolitical industrial base. This will go against the grain of how the United States drew down its defence industry with the famous "last supper" and reduced the size of the contractor pool. It also goes against the legacy of the past twenty years of those prime contractors outsourcing key parts and subsystems to a national or, many times, global supply chain.

We are talking about major change in the United States, Australia, Europe, and Japan to recognise that having surge production capability is more important than simply narrow control of markets. The 20 May 2025, agreement between President Biden and Prime Minister Albanese is clearly a step in the right direction. "The President plans to ask the United States Congress to add Australia as a 'domestic source' within the meaning of Title III of the Defence Production Act. Doing so would streamline technological and industrial base collaboration, accelerate and strengthen AUKUS implementation, and build new opportunities for United States investment in the production and purchase of Australian critical minerals, critical technologies, and other strategic sectors."[7]

---

6. https://www.wsj.com/articles/seeking-a-bigger-bang-u-s-inves
   ts-in-advanced-explosives-7239e5fb

7. https://www.whitehouse.gov/briefing-room/statements-release
   s/2023/05/20/australia-united-states-joint-leaders-statement-an
   -alliance-for-our-times/

An April 2023 discussion with Dr. Alan Dupont provided some important insight on how to shape a way ahead with regard to Australian defence industry and the challenge of shaping an allied arsenal of democracy. We argued that discussing sustainability in terms of a defence industrial base is too narrow an approach. It really is about shaping the entire eco-system for sustainable defence forces, which includes specific defence companies, new acquisition approaches, companies that support the core capabilities which defence taps into but are not specifically defence companies per se and tapping into new logistical and support approaches to support distributed force. As Dupont underscored: "I think we should move away from this defence industrial base language which can be very clunky and twentieth century. People think in terms of big factories and production and development cycles of 20 years. We need a very different focus."

Dupont laid out a methodology for building what he considers to be an appropriate Australian defence industrial effort. As it stands now, Australia is almost entirely dependent on overseas supplies and when Australia orders what it needs, it joins the queue along with other customers, with no certainty to be supplied in a timely manner. Add to this the tyranny of distance facing the transportation of military parts to Australia, and you have a perfect storm facing the Australian defence in terms of conflict.

To deal with this challenge, Australia needs to enhance its sovereign defence production capabilities. But to do so, Dupont suggests the need for a realistic methodology to shape the way ahead.

What does Australia need in terms of defence capabilities over the next two decades? How much of what it needs could realistically be produced in Australia? What can it do with co-development or co-production with key allies? And what will it simply have to procure from allied countries and producers?

In those areas where it is feasible to build sovereign capabilities, a new development approach is needed. Many of the dynamic new capabilities being used by defence forces come from smaller, more innovative firms. Australia has such firms but there is no Australian government policy to support them or to ensure that they have the capital to grow. There is a need for an Australian industrial policy in this area.

In areas where Australia could produce for its own needs, the government should commit to a South Korean, Israeli, or Swedish path of growing for exports. He pointed out that South Korea now exports 17 billion dollars' worth of exports which provides a key pillar for its own defence.

In addition, to discussing his methodology for the development of Australian sovereign defence industrial capabilities, we discussed the strategic direction of defence and how best to support it. Defence forces in the Pacific for the liberal democracies are focusing on force distribution for survivability.

There are new technologies to support force distribution such as synthetic fuel production and 3D printing in the field. New approaches to sustaining distributed forces through a relevant development and production support are crucial to providing enhanced capabilities for distributed forces.

New platform/payload combinations are being introduced through such sectors as aerial and maritime autonomous systems. How will Australia support this effort? How will it do so in a way that allows for exportability? How will it work with core allies to enhance the rapidity of change in this area? Cost effective and expendable platforms carrying a variety of payloads are a key element of the new defence equipment ecosystem. How will this ecosystem be supported and thrive? Most likely, not with old acquisition approaches and older concepts of a "defence industrial base."

A reworking of the Australian approach to supplying its forces is required. But it should be done in a realistic manner but with a focus on the force structure changes taking place and the need to help sustain a distributed defence force both now and in the future.

"Impactful Projection"

The DSR argues for what it calls "impactful projection" for the ADF. This is how the DSR characterises the requirement: "The defence of Australia lies in the collective security of the Indo-Pacific. The defence of Australia's national interests lies in the protection of our economic connection with the world and the maintenance of the global rules-based order.

"Accordingly, the Australian Defence Force (ADF) must have the capacity to:

- defend Australia and our immediate region;

- deter through denial any adversary's attempt to project power against Australia through our northern approaches;

- protect Australia's economic connection to our region and the world;

- contribute with our partners to the collective security of the Indo-Pacific; and

- contribute with our partners to the maintenance of the global rules-based order.

"As most of these objectives lie well beyond our borders, the ADF must have the capacity to engage in impactful projection across the full spectrum of proportionate response. The ADF must be able to hold an adversary at risk further from our shores."

But this gets again at the geography and effects problem. Which geography can the ADF operate from and within and generate enough impact to make a difference against the Chinese?

Personally, I think this breaks down into two different answers. The first is what the ADF can do operating with the United States or Japanese forces or both deep in the Pacific from Australia's point of view but closer to Chinese military actions in either their first or second island chain? And secondly, how capable is the ADF to operate by building defence in depth within Australia and then operating up to and including its first island chain?

The key element or capability for doing either operational matrix is the capability of the C2/ISR networks to support ADF operations both nationally and in coalition. The longer the range, the harder the challenge and the more likely the ADF is to face significant threats to the viability of those networks. The closer to China the targeted weapons are to come, the absolute imperative for Australia and American targeting to be integrated, for the simple fact that conventional long-range strikes are inherently related to the questions of the run up to nuclear deterrence. There is no hard break between targeting an adversaries C2/ISR systems for longer range strike conventionally and the spill over into nuclear use issues.

Paul Bracken has put this challenge rather clearly. In an article published in *The Hill*, Bracken underscored the threat of inadvertent use of new technologies for conventional modernisation upon escalation management.

"Failure to think about new military technologies makes it more likely that these systems could be used in reckless ways and, if used, could lead to unplanned escalation. It is important to take this problem seriously, because we are in the early stage of a long-term arms race with advanced technologies such as artificial intelligence (AI), hypersonic missiles, cyber weapons, drones, *and the like . . .*

"Drones, cyber, AI, hypersonic missiles, anti-satellite attack and other advanced technologies are central to U.S. long-term competition with China and Russia. Some of these technologies have spread to North Korea and Iran. These two nations, for example, already are major threats in cyber war, and both operate armed drones.

"Here we see the new escalation problem facing the United States. Using these technologies against terrorists and insurgents, or to disrupt a weak power such as Iran's uranium enrichment, the chances of a large eruption in violence by an enemy's response are low. Terrorists and insurgents lack the weapons to strike back at the United States in a meaningful way.

"But used against China, Russia or North Korea, the risk is altogether different. Even in a limited war with conventional weapons the new technologies could become highly destabilizing. More, these are nuclear-weapon states. In peacetime, China, Russia and North Korea do a good job of controlling their nuclear forces. There are no reports of accidents or unintended missile launches by any of them. They are cautious and disciplined when it comes to these weapons.

"But this is in peacetime—caution and discipline are easy because there are no stresses on their leadership or military command systems.

"Crises and limited wars aren't like that. In an intense crisis or limited war, all bets are off—or, at least, all bets need to be recalculated. And this is the point: Any policy review needs to assess the escalation potential of their use. Basing reviews on the way they are used against

terrorists and insurgents overlooks the critical difference that heavily armed nations bring to the problem. They can strike back at the United States or its allies, and this ability calls for a different type of review that goes beyond collateral damage. It must focus on the likelihood of counter-escalation.

"To control escalation, the United States must take account of the fog of war not only in our own forces, but in the enemy forces as well. Against a nuclear weapon state, the United States isn't simply taking out targets; it is playing a larger game of mutual risk-taking. Any review that ignores this point misses the essence of the decision facing U.S. leaders."[8]

The DSR highlights two new acquisitions which are designed to give Australia a seat at the table in making decisions about "impactful projection" involving long-range strikes, namely the acquisition of SSNs and of Tomahawk missiles. Australia is acquiring up to 220 Tomahawk Land Attack Missiles and will be the first country outside of the U.S. and the UK to acquire them and these weapons will be integrated into the Royal Australian Navy's Hobart-class destroyers.

The other part of "impactful projection" from my point of view even more significant in dealing with the Chinese challenge is to provide for Australia's direct defence and enhanced capabilities to operate from its own territory and up to and including the Australian first island chain.

8.

https://thehill.com/opinion/national-security/543023-the-risk-of-new-military-technologies-must-be-properly-assessed/.
Also, see
https://defence.info/re-thinking-strategy/2021/03/conventional-forces-and-technology-what-is-their-impact-on-escalation-management-with-nuclear-powers/

As Brian Weston suggested in a 2020 series of articles on the Williams Foundation website but which were originally published by the Australian Defence Business Review: "The notion of Australia's First Island Chain brings a clearer conceptual basis for force development and operational planning, a lesser dependence on the complexities and national interests of partners and allies and yet, the region remains of critical relevance to Australia's security. So, is Australia capitalising on these realities by devoting enough effort to the detail of how Australia can defend and dominate the nation's 'Red Zone'?"[9]

Doing so is very challenging for the current ADF but several of the pieces of the SDR, if implemented, could well allow the Australian nation, for the ADF by itself is not enough to be able to do so, to operate from its own territory, notably from the North. This has the other advantage of providing a mobile sanctuary for the core allies of Australia to reinforce their ability to fight in a crisis in terms of sustainment and support, as well as working effective coalition operations with partners in the region.

But doing both—a significant commitment to long-range strike and an ability to build out the defence of the nation's Red Zone—is frankly far beyond the current budget commitments of the current government. There is also the really critical question of the C2/ISR capabilities to operate a force at distance versus one leveraging one's continent projecting out into the red zone.

The challenge of such a build out can be seen in the case of one program which can provide for both Red Zone operations and support longer range strike, but will not be enough by itself, namely, the Triton program. Wing Commander Keirin Joyce, Program Chief Engineer

---

9. https://defense.info/re-thinking-strategy/2020/09/defending-so uth-of-australias-first-island-chain/

RPAS (MQ-4C Triton) for the RAAF, highlighted in an interview in April 2023 that with the US Navy and the RAAF both operating the Triton, working cooperative operations can clearly be envisaged as Australia and the US Navy will compliment areas of operations of significance to both countries to enhance the ISR/C2 capabilities of both. And as the ADF builds out its longer-range strike capabilities, having the Triton as an asset to assist in the targeting process will be important as well.

Triton comes at a key time in the evolution of ADF capabilities to enable longer-range effects from Australia out into the region. But Joyce commented that what will be interesting to note 'is this enough?' He thinks Australia will need even more assets, and uncrewed/automated/autonomous assets are probably the answer in the current challenging climate of attracting and retaining workforce."

If one gets specific and concrete about what capabilities the ADF has to operate with and where it must operate, I think one needs to think in terms of impacts on the Chinese military and not just long-range strike. Without doubt, it is important to have national long-range strike precisely to give Australia a seat at the table in the case of broader conflict in the Pacific. But this reminds more of the years of work I have done with the French on the question of influencing the Americans to do the right thing from their point of view in European defence and having their independent nuclear deterrent as a means to do so. Having independent long-range strike is currently conceived as the functional equivalent for Australian influence strategy.

A very good discussion of the options for long-range strike for the ADF was provided in the Williams Foundation Seminar on the subject, held on 22 August 2018. In that seminar, Michael Shoebridge, director of ASPI's Defence, Strategy and National Security program, focused on the problem in a way not discussed by the SDR but central to the reality of how Australia builds out a long-strike capability.

Shoebridge argued: "The intimidation effect of a nuclear armed state is sufficiently great that this seems to me to be very likely indeed to stop an Australian Prime Minister from using offensive strike beyond Australia's territories. To take a pretty clear example, the idea of posturing to reach out and touch Beijing's leaders with precision conventional weapons just seems outlandish to me as anything but a way of ensuring a destructive counterstrike that is not conventional.

"This does put aside the question of how then to directly strike Chinese forces operating in the region, and how to separate the threat of nuclear use from an ability of Australia to defend itself and work with allies to stop the Chinese in their tracks to not only project power into the region but use it.

"What then? Kinetic strike is not the only kind that can deter others. The rise of the cyber world has created a new potential form of long-range strike: offensive cyber. The attraction of this new capability is its global reach and its uncertainty; this kind of logic will be very familiar to the submariners in the audience. The value of uncertainty about where a cyber capability is and what it might be prepared to affect makes it a tool of potentially large importance in the world of deterrence.

"Yet its opacity and uncertainty can also reduce its value. And cyber tools tend to be boutique things that take a lot of preparation, but once revealed can be countered fairly rapidly. So, the problem of how to signal capability without exposing it is one that is still to be worked out.

"A further limitation on broad use of offensive cyber for strike is that containing the effect is not simple—think of the StuxNet virus that seems to have been intended for limited use on a non-internet connected system, but went beyond that, and of the cyber disruption brought about by Wannacry and NotPetya.

"Even within kinetic strike, Australia might have options other than air launched. "Pre-positioned Army units with ground launched anti-ship and aircraft systems could work with regional partners to strike adversary forces at a distance from Australia. Australia's new naval combatants—surface and sub-surface—might be equipped with cruise missiles or missile systems that fit into the launcher cells of ships. These require pre-positioning. The option of air-delivered lethal effect at range needs to be considered along with such other strike options.

"The good news is that any offensive strike capability Australia might consider needs many similar underpinning enablers and capabilities if it is to be targeted effectively and if decisions on use are to be made well. Among the enablers will be strong policy frameworks that put the posturing of strike and its potential use within a broader strategic framework.

"Long-range strike if emphasized would thus be in a context, and if it involved direct confrontation with China, the U.S. would very much be involved and hence it boils down to finding ways to make sure extended deterrence as well as credible conventional options to influence Chinese thinking."[10]

Working in the Neighbourhood

---

10. Robbin Laird, Joint by Design: The Evolution of Australian Defence Strategy (pp. 243–244), Kindle Edition.

The ability to work effectively in the neighbourhood from a military point of view starts with building a more resilient Australia within which the military can operate and be sustained as a sanctuary from which to project forces in the region. This is a major task which if pursued as a priority will take time, effort, innovation, and investments.

Technology will be part of such an effort. Building secure telecommunications channels that can be used in a crisis, the use of new and innovative ways such as using UAVs for delivery systems to bare bases and locations, and the use of USVs and UUVs to create ISR grids which can feed into diversified C2 networks for the command of distributed forces are examples illustrating what a comprehensive effort would look like.

The build out of locations from which repairs can be performed for military equipment, including ships and airplanes, will require innovation in terms of new ways such as 3D printing to allow for a more diversified set of locations from which to do so for both the ADF and allied militaries.

The Maritime Border Command works closely with partners in the neighbourhood to work the many issues involved in shared situational awareness and joint operations to provide for security to Australia from the sea.[11] This could be expanded into new information sharing with the neighbours in terms of basic security and maritime awareness through shared acquisition of USVs and sharing of information generated from these USVs. Currently, the Australian government is using an Australian company to build USVs generating ISR informa-

---

11. https://sldinfo.com/2019/05/australian-sovereignty-and-mariti me-security-radm-goddard-discusses-the-role-of-the-maritime-b order-command/

tion useful for such tasks.[12] Why not build out shared builds, shared operations, and shared data to work an ISR grid for security awareness across the region?

To provide for the maritime and air security of Australia, a build-up of ISR capability and associated C2 is underway. Why not expand this capability by using the new generation of USVs, UUVs, and UAVs which are being tested, developed, and built? By building a dense network of surveillance to support the Australian sanctuary, there is the added benefit of doing so to aid allies in terms of crisis as well to provide support for rotational allied forces.

Such an approach has important effects on the build out of the services and the joint force. The RAAF remains the tip of the spear. There is no element of military power more capable of signalling to an adversary your early involvement in a crisis or shaping a deterrent effect than airpower. The question will be how to bulk up the deterrent effect from the manned element of the force and at greater distance. But airpower has the flexibility of providing a rapid scaled effect.

The resilience challenge comes into play here. How will Australia have adequate strike capabilities? How to build or store adequate munitions for the force? The answer in part is using Australia's unique test ranges in a broader alliance effort to build out a new generation of missiles which are built jointly with the United States and like-minded

---

12.

https://sldinfo.com/2023/05/maritime-autonomous-systems-p
roviding-mission-threads-for-australian-defence-and-security-th
e-case-of-the-bluebottle-usv/

states. The example of what Norway has done with the Naval Strike missile is one to be considered by Australia.[13]

The Australians have stood up a weapons enterprise, but it will need to do much more than being a conduit for importing extant American missiles. It needs to become a fulcrum for generating change in the weapons side of the equation for Australia and by so doing for the broader set of alliance partners of Australia.

The Royal Australian Navy faces a major challenge in terms of sorting out the mix and match platforms within the operating force. But the way ahead in my view for the maritime force is to operate within a kill-web ecosystem where ships can both contribute to and benefit from third-party targeting to develop distributed but integrated firing solutions.

This was underscored in an interview I did with the U.S. Navy sub commander in an interview conducted in Honolulu in April 2023. Rear Admiral Jablon underscored the nature of the shift as follows: "The submarine force is now becoming part of the 'combat clusters' that you're talking about instead of an independent operator. In the Cold War, we operated independently, alone, and unafraid. During the land wars, we started becoming part of the joint force as we provided land fires via the TLAM. Now, we are fully integrated with the joint force in terms of targeting and communications. But, of course, we can also conduct independent operations as the 'silent service' when directed."[14]

---

13. https://sldinfo.com/2022/11/nsm-and-jsm-a-norwegian-contri bution-to-the-arsenal-of-democracy/

14. https://sldinfo.com/2023/05/rear-admiral-jeffrey-jablon-on-the -u-s-pacific-submarine-force/

But what capital ships can Australia build and maintain effectively? What class of ships? What will be the interaction between these capital ships and autonomous systems? There is a whole world of innovation in the maritime domain underway which Australia must tap into because of its limited manpower and manufacturing resources.

Rather than taking a platform replacement perspective or build strategy, the focus needs to shift to a distributed but integratable kill-web ecosystem within which ships can operate. This is where innovation can be driven in the rapidly evolving robotic world.

Rather than seeing autonomous systems in the short- or medium-term creating ghost fleets, their role will be to expand the range, capability, and lethality of capital assets. Rather than looking simply at the organic capability on a specific platform, we will consider surface ships using such capabilities as becoming mother ships and submarines will share in this development as well. But then how to build ships in a world altered by the arrival of USVs, UUVs, and UAVs?

And how will the rebuild of the fleet interact with the strategic shift in terms of the Australian Army? The Australian Army given its operation of the land is the key force in terms of working in the neighbourhood. Re-thinking Army's role which has been called for in the SDR is closely connected with defining what the defence perimeter for Australian direct defence is and how best for the ADF to operate in that space.

In a 2022 interview which John Blackburn and I had with John Blaxland, we discussed this issue and its impact on the way ahead for the ADF. We focused on what we agreed most logically defined the defence perimeter: operations from the continent to Australia's first island chain, which is outward from the continent to the Solomon Islands and across to Papua New Guinea, Timor L'este, and Indonesia.

This is how Blaxland defined how to shape an approach for this strategic space with the ADF operating an appropriate manoeuvre force supported by appropriate infrastructure in Northern and Western Australia which could support such a force. "We need to be mindful of our history and our geography and our neighborhood is a neighborhood with a history of violence. When we faced existential challenges in the past, we have had to forward deploy into the island chain to Australia's north."

He argued that the initial efforts to project such a force did not work out all that well in the early years of World War II but by 1944, Australia had sorted out a more effective capability to operate outward into the first island chain. He noted: "When we faced an existential crisis in 1942, it came through the archipelago, through Indonesia, through Papua New Guinea and the Solomon Islands. That is increasingly contested space today, and it's all the more important that we invest in a strategy that capitalizes on the relationships with those countries in the archipelago. From a force structure point of view, that means actually thinking about how we structure our forces to enable deployment in that space and to operate alongside the neighbours, but in a contested environment."

As a former Army officer, he discussed how he saw the future of the Army working with the joint force in the strategic space defined by operating from the continent to the first island chain. He argued that defence diplomacy coupled with an enhanced ability of the Army to operate forward in support of the air and sea forces was critical.

To project airpower at range likely would require maintenance of lily pad–like forward operating bases for which a ground force has an important defensive role—including capabilities that would ensure overmatch against a would-be adversary—including mobile, protected armoured platforms with the ability to reach out and touch someone at range.

With regard to defence diplomacy, this is what he underscored: "We have for the last two decades basically been distracted by operations in the Middle East, what I call our niche wars in Afghanistan and Iraq. We've dropped the ball in terms of building relationships, understanding the culture, the language, the people, the networks in our neighborhood. We are starting to reinvest in that space, but we've got a long way to go. Very few of our seniors and our middle level commanders and managers speak the relevant languages, for example."

He argued that "we have designed a force to plug and play with the Americans, but that is not what we need for the future. Interoperability with the Americans remains important for sure, but Australia needs to be able to conduct its own operations in the neighborhood in a self-reliant manner, as well as alongside neighbours."

What this also means is that Northern and Western Australia need to see significant infrastructure development to sustain and operate such a force. And frankly, this is a whole of government issue, and not just about what the Department of Defence can fund.

Such a shift towards enhanced capabilities for direct defence of Australia clearly has implications for core allies like Japan and the United States. Blaxland argued that "the best thing we can do is make Australia more self-reliant, more resilient, more able to defend its own turf, and collaborate with neighbors to defend our common strategic space." "If Australia provides a firm base, and if we have a leavening effect on our own neighborhood, then that takes away the stress of planning for others who might be thinking about other contingencies, and a key point to my mind is this is all about deterring war, deterring the prospects of war. We need to dissuade adventures from competitors and would-be adversaries while being reared to fight and win when deterrence fails."[15]

All of this leave a significant impact on the way ahead for the Australian Army. It plays a key role within Australia but what is the government asking it to do going forward? And what is it willing to invest in so that it could do so?

A key implication of the shift to the neighbourhood is finding ways for the Army to move from Australian territory to areas within the neighbourhood where it might need to go. With a significant shortfall on lift—sea or air—how will this happen? What kind of RAN will be built to support this? How will Army aviation be able to move quickly if it continues to not have access to tiltrotor which has revolutionised the ability of the USMC to move ground forces rapidly across the Pacific chessboard?

In my interview with the chief of Army in April 2023, Lieutenant General Stuart Simon provided some of the answers which he thought the Army could provide for the strategic shift. Lieutenant General Stuart spoke at some length to the territorial presence role of the Australian Army as underwriting the ability for direct defence and shaping an effective foundation for joint force power projection from Australia.[16]

"At the foundation and during my presentation, we emphasized the importance of being able to leverage Australian geography for strategic purposes. The Army is located in 157 locations around the country,

---

15. https://sldinfo.com/2022/09/prioritizing-the-direct-defence-of
    -australia-shaping-a-way-ahead-for-the-adf/

16. https://sldinfo.com/2023/05/the-role-of-the-australian-army-i
    n-the-way-ahead-for-australian-deterrence-strategy/

from the most northern tip of Cape York to Tasmania and from the west to the east coast. And our connection into local towns, cities and communities is through these 157 locations where our people are located. One of the key design principles for our Army Objective Force is what we call the total workforce system. We have a flexible set of arrangements for people to work full or part time or a combination of both throughout their career in the Army. That helps us have a workforce in 157 locations, as some of these are sparsely populated.

"Our capacity to leverage our total workforce system means we can leverage our part time brigades to project force from the bases South of the Tropic of Capricorn into the northern geography to reinforce and protect our sustainment capabilities in that part of the country. We have restructured our 2nd Division to be a division which leverages our total workforce system. Its six formations leverage our part time people in great part."

With recent natural disasters in Australia, such as the bush fires, the Army has been mobilised to help the nation in non-defence crises. This has meant that C2 has been used for national mobilisation as well as to transport equipment to move force to the point of need. There is the challenge of overtaxing the Army for such tasks, but it does suggest that mobilisation is a whole of nation effort, not simply a tip of the spear warfighting support effort.

We then discussed one aspect of mobilisation which has become clearly evident, namely a relationship between government and industry to provide for war materiel at levels of effectiveness and not just in time efficiencies. Alan Dupont and others spoke at the 28 March Williams seminar on the impact of the Ukraine War which has demonstrated the absence of the kind of arsenal of democracy which Australia and the liberal democracies need.

We did discuss the munitions challenge which requires significant investment in development and the buying of weapons stockpiles. With regard to Australia, Lieutenant General Stuart noted: "We need to have the capacity to store, maintain, and perform upgrades on guided weapons in Australia using an Australian workforce. And that is a prerequisite to the capacity to then be able to either provide component manufacture or assembly or actually to manufacture guided weapons and explosive ordnance in the country."

For Lieutenant General Stuart, the Australian Army has a key role to play in the way ahead for the direct defence of Australia and the role of the ADF and the Australian nation in the region. Doing so will take imagination, resources, and commitment—qualities which are always in short supply, at least in my view.

Mobilisation

The way ahead on Australian defence entails a whole of government and a whole of society challenge, notably in terms of how defence had changed with the multi-faceted threats which China poses to Australia and the liberal democratic global order.

To prepare and respond requires a mobilisation strategy. With the wildfire and pandemic crises, Australia faced significant challenges which required mobilisation and broader social awareness. The demand signal notably on the Army has been very high in recent years and has impacted the force. It is clear that the Army being present throughout Australia is well positioned to spearhead such efforts but frankly should not be given the primary task of staffing out the entire effort.

This requires shaping a mobilisation system available for social, natural, and environmental crises and available in times of need for national defence. Mobilisation in this sense is not strictly a defence term but rather one which needs to be understood as a broader requirement for how society is evolving in the age of various challenges. And public involvement is crucial to shape the kind of awareness required to have a fully supported approach by the nation to resilience. The need is for robust resilience, not reticent resistance.

In an interview with Air Marshal John Harvey (Retired) after his presentation at the March 2023 Williams Foundation Seminar, we discussed the importance of shaping an effective mobilisation system as part of the way forward for Australian defence. Harvey underscored that what was required in the new context was a whole of government, society, and whole of alliance capability.

With regard to mobilisation, he made the very sound point that mobilisation was important across the whole of government and society to deal with a variety of challenges, not just defence. Indeed, if one correlated mobilisation simply with defence, that would lead to failure to focus on the much broader challenge which is best characterised by a capability for national resilience. From this point of view, deterrence then is based on social cohesion and national cohesion to sustain Australia through the pressures which the changing global system puts upon her.

The broader need for mobilisation is the engagement and involvement of the citizenry in the protection, health, viability, and defence of their island continent. It is not a task for the ADF as a boutique force at the service of the tasks given to it by the prime minister of the day. When one considers the breadth of the shift in defence posed by a multi-domain, multi-spectre, and cross domain authoritarian world redefining power such as China, the engagement of the Australian citizenry to participate in the overall defence of Australia is not a nice one but a fundamental one.[17]

In addition to the broader set of national challenges, the specific focus on the imperative of creating in the Northern Territory the right kind of infrastructure to support direct defence and "impactful projection" requires mobilisation of national resources for a region with scarce populations and infrastructure to support such efforts.

Glenn Brown and John Coyne precisely made these points in their 28 April 2023, which they entitled, *Turning the defence review into action will require a major mobilisation.*

"Northern Australia's critical transport infrastructure has multiple single points of failure that create strategic vulnerabilities. The logistics and supply chain networks to and from northern Australia are already subject to and stressed by weather-driven disruptions.

"Northern Australia's economy has limited market depth and surge capacity, so completing major new works requires engagement across multiple government agencies and market sectors, and awareness of the coming waves of large-scale resource projects in the Territory and their massive impacts on the 'normal' economy and supply chains of people and products. The DSR mentions tapping into the civilian and mining infrastructures of the north. That's commendable but it means that energy and minerals sector players will become 'interested parties' and must join the planning cohorts.

"The NT, like all the states and territories, has a significant housing shortage. Achieving the DSR goals will require significantly large work forces who will need to be housed. This must be addressed as a priority.

---

17. https://defense.info/featured-story/2023/05/sigint-cyber-infor mation-war-and-21st-century-deterrence/

"Defence will need to assess what the force posture changes in northern Australia will require of the ADF, and state and territory governments, defence industry and the construction community.

"In addition to defence and minerals commitments, these demands appear likely to present serious challenges along with the need for facilities for visiting U.S. and Japanese personnel. What happens next and how the guidance of the DSR translates into operational plans and tactics will be significant undertakings that all the stakeholders will need to support. This will require the largest mobilisation effort in Australia since World War II."[18]

The general perception that defence is a task for professionals and not of the citizenry has become cemented in all of the liberal democracies with the exception of the Baltic states, the Nordics, and the Poles. But this "citizenry gap" is a crucial challenge facing Australia along with its major allies.

Or as Scott Davidson put it in an article published on 1 March 2023:

"Like many Western societies, there has been an increasing gap in Australia between militaries and the societies they represent. Since the abolition of National Service in Australia in 1972—midway through the Vietnam War—the impact of wars after the end of the Cold War have not affected society directly. The wars of choice since World War II removed the requirement for mass mobilisation or defence spending. Australian spending on the military through the last 20 years never exceeded 6% of the Federal budget. This minimises the tangible impact on the population of a nation at war; such as increases in

---

18. https://www.aspistrategist.org.au/turning-the-defence-review-into-action-will-require-a-major-mobilisation/

taxation, government directed shifts in industry, or national rationing of critical resources.

"The enduring nature of war and the approach China might apply to major conflict in the Indo-Pacific means future war for Australia will likely be protracted and costly. Even if the theatres of battle are distant from Australia, the economic disruption from war in the Indo-Pacific would be significant due to the economic interdependence from globalisation. Arguably, the impact on societies would be broader than previous instances of total war in the twentieth century, even without considering the threat of nuclear weapons.

"The dependence of civilian society on the two new domains of war, cyber and space, means that regardless of how governments may try to insulate their society from the cost of war, there will be impacts on the modern conveniences that people today take for granted. This impact added on top of the other costs of war would exacerbate the vulnerability to Maoist Protracted War, with the Australian population increasingly unwilling to endure a long, costly, drawn-out war which undermines their standard of living.

"Australians have lost the experience of privation and national mobilisation that contributed to success in World War II. The current focus on prioritising social comfort over national security and shielding populations from the costs associated with war, undermines the resilience of the population to endure and accept privation associated with an existential conflict. This is natural when the threat is low.

"However, the status quo has changed and so should Australian's mindsets. Compare Australia's current posture with the preparations in China of hardened communication systems, reserves of fuel and logistics, and a strong ideology rooted in a national narrative that has prepared the Chinese population for a protracted struggle."[19]

The Nuclear Factor

Overhanging any consideration of the way ahead for Australian defence is the nuclear factor. And it impacts in three different ways. The first way is the coming of the nuclear submarine to the Royal Australian Navy. Here, not only will the RAN receive, then build and operate nuclear submarines, but they will work with the United States and the United Kingdom and perhaps France in hosting their own nuclear submarines when doing patrols in the Pacific.

As Vice Admiral Mead noted, Australia will build operating facilities for these submarines and have the security systems which the United States considers necessary to protect them. And this means building a base on Australian soil which could raise domestic objections against the critical claims of those Australians who have historically opposed nuclear power and its use on Australian soil, not the least of which has been past historical statements and positions taken by the current Prime Minister.

Divisions within the Labour Party and the role of the Greens in the Australian political system will make opposition to things nuclear even including the AUKUS submarines a factor going forward. And given the nature of the Australian system of federal government, the power of the Australian left will raise questions as well of where the base or bases are located and with what political effect.

---

19. https://theforge.defence.gov.au/publications/can-australians-fight

Does political division pop up at a later point to threaten the AUKUS submarine deal?

The second way is the crucial question of Australia's ability to deal with energy resilience. Australia has both abundant coal and uranium but policies support diminishing reliance on coal and not the use of uranium going forward. Australia could, if it so chose, be energy independent largely due to its ability to tap into solar and nuclear energy sources, and with a significant rebuild of the electric power grid.[20] But there seems to be little appetite to go the nuclear energy route for energy generation.

But how will Australia have enough energy sources, most notably fossil fuels, in times of an enduring crisis? And how will it ensure that it has enough merchant shipping to bring supplies into the country during such a period?

To operate their submarines, Australia will build a generation of nuclear power officers. But unlike in the United States or France, these officers will not operate against the background of a broader domestic nuclear power engineering sector. Presumably, domestic capabilities of some sort will have to be created for training. But this is a glass half full when it comes to realising the benefits of nuclear power generation for an energy independence stance in Australia.

But regardless of a position on domestic nuclear power, Australia and its allies face three nuclear powers in the region and possessing

---

20. And building a grid that can be protected against various attacks including cyber ones. See the following: https://defence.info/re-thinking-strategy/2019/12/infrastructu re-defence-as-a-key-element-of-national-security-policy-securing -americas-electric-grid/

nuclear weapons does matter in shaping one's posture of operating conventional forces.

That nuclear deterrence affects conventional operations has been obvious in the war in Ukraine. But that war has raised questions about the spillover effect into the Pacific. I wrote a piece published on 9 April 2023, which highlighted the impact of nuclear deterrence on the sanctuaries of rear support for the war which underscored how nuclear weapons play into conventional operations even if they are not directly used, which is a key consideration for any consideration of ADF use in a conflict with China.

"There are many aspects of the war being studied by militaries worldwide, but one aspect of the conflict is dramatically evident—the war is fueled by supplies from the West delivered by supply lines from the West into Ukraine and supplies from Russian territory into Ukraine supporting Russian forces. There is evident concern to avoid striking either rear area and there can be little explanation other than the fear of escalation why this is so. And the escalation at risk is a threat of nuclear use. Does anyone really believe the Russians would tolerate this if not for British nuclear deterrence reinforced by the American nuclear force?

"As Paul Bracken has noted: 'Someone called me yesterday to ask if the Russians would actually use nuclear weapons. My response was "they already have." It's a nuclear head game, and very dangerous.

"The purpose of the Russian nuclear alert is to deter NATO from massing its forces against Belarus and Ukraine borders. And to signal that the U.S. had better not open up a big electronic warfare or cyber campaign to disrupt Russian Air Forces over Ukraine.

"A U.S. or NATO cyber campaign against distributed tactical nuclear and mobile missiles of Russia would manipulate the risk of escalation, which is why Putin ordered the alert.'

"But there is a growing danger of escalation. On the Western side, prior to the war, there was a de facto expectation that the West could trade space for time in a Russian attack on NATO. But no state that borders Russia (and now we have a new one in NATO), watching the atrocities the Russians have committed in Ukrainian territory, can want to trade space for time. This could well mean that these border states want long-range strike weapons as part of their arsenal along with more credible air and missile defence capabilities.

"And such long-range weapons can be land or air-based and are being built in the West to deal with the distances in the Pacific to deal with the China challenge. Additionally, the Ukrainians have reputedly asked for longer range missiles which would allow them to hit Russian supply areas deeper into Russia.

"The Russians can contemplate various ways chemical weapons could be used against supply chains operating within Ukraine from the West. Does the West have sufficient defensive capability to keep the supply chain rolling in such circumstances? Does the West have a realistic offensive answer?

"But the core question is simply put: does the possession of nuclear weapons effectively create sanctuaries in your territory in case of conflict? Does this work with regard to extended deterrence as well by the United States with its allies? Would this apply to the defence of Australia as it expands its basing support for the United States? Does this work as well in the Pacific with China, Russia, North Korea and the mainland of the United States effectively operating as sanctuaries because of their nuclear arsenals? How does the question affect warfighting strategies, muti-domain or otherwise?

"And most of all, the drive toward expanded numbers of nuclear states envisaged in Bracken's second nuclear age is hardly undercut by the Ukraine War experience to date. It is most likely a positive proof of the need to do so by a major state."[21]

This last point raises the key question of whether other states in the Pacific region will decide to become nuclear weapons states, such as South Korea. Australia could see its defence position complicated by proliferation in the region spawned by events in Europe, Iran, and North Korea and in ways that complicate the credibility of American nuclear deterrence policy.

And that is the elephant in the room—American extended nuclear deterrence. Professor Stephan Frühling co-authored a piece published in *Survival* on 4 February 2022, which precisely looked at the necessity and the path whereby U.S. extended deterrence could be enhanced in the face of the Chinese nuclear build-up. As they noted: "Forward-based nuclear forces are a central element in coupling allied and U.S. security, creating risks of entanglement for the adversary and addressing adversary threats of limited use. NATO has such forces. In the NPR, the U.S. should present for consideration the possibility of forward-basing nuclear weapons in the Indo-Pacific, as well as stationing dual-capable aircraft there, perhaps including some with South Korean and Japanese crews that are certified to carry out nuclear missions.

"Given the relative lack of strategic buffer between South Korea and North Korea, and between China and the southern islands of Japan, even relatively short-range dual-capable aircraft systems could fulfil an important coupling role. As an operational expression of Washington's willingness to give allies some say in the avoidance of nuclear

---

21. https://defense.info/highlight-of-the-week/the-war-in-ukraine
-and-the-sanctuaries-of-rear-support-the-impact-of-nuclear-det
errence/

sanctuaries during a conflict, such forces would compel adversaries to take seriously the role of U.S. nuclear capabilities in a major conflict. This dispensation would introduce escalation risks that China currently does not face into any counterforce campaign against the U.S. and its allies."[22]

In the 1980s, I spent an enormous amount of time on this issue, notably in the context of the Euro-missile crisis. I did much research and published many articles and books on the French and British nuclear arsenals and their relationships with what the United States might contribute in a theatre war. This subject has returned with a vengeance and simply cannot be ignored when looking at the question of deterrence in the Pacific against a mature nuclear power like China combined with a personal nuclear arsenal possessed by the leader of North Korea or the question of how Russia and its war in Ukraine will affect its own nuclear posture.

This is hardly a historical study but living history so to speak.

I will conclude this section and this chapter with a look at the critical nuclear issue provided by Frühling at a 2018 Williams Foundation seminar that focused on long-range strike. This is what I wrote in a 19 September 2018, article:

"How does the return of the nuclear dimension and evolving U.S. policy affect Australian options and ways ahead?

"At the recent Williams Foundation seminar on independent strike, one of the speakers, Dr. Stephen Frühling from the Strategic and Defence Studies Centre of the Australian National University, provided an insightful look at the options and impacts upon Australia of the

---

22. Stephan Frühling and Andrew O'Neil, "Alliances and Nuclear Risk: Strengthening US Extended Deterrence" Survival (4 February, 2022, p. 92).

new strategic situation. His presentation *Australian Strike Capability and Nuclear Deterrence* follows:

"'It's certainly remarkable that nuclear weapons have made a return to Australia's defence debate, if you can call this what's going on in the relevant blogosphere, not least following more or less subtle hints by Hugh White, Paul Dibb and Richard Brabin-Smith that Australia might need to consider looking at relevant lead-times again, in the way the Defence Committee recommended to Governments from the late 1950s to the last Strategic Basis Paper of 1983.*

"'Australian nuclear weapons is not what I will discuss today, however, although I might point you to an upcoming edition of Australian Foreign Policy, available in your well-stocked neighbourhood bookstore, for more on that issue.*

"'That said, the question of what circumstances and to what end Australia might acquire nuclear weapons is an interesting one, since it really draws us to think about when not just our current force and posture, but also credible increases and a conventional posture in general would be stretched to a breaking point—and that certainly is of relevance to discussing the future of Australian independent strike.*

"'But the current revival of interest in nuclear weapons is real, and it goes far beyond Australia—if anything, I would say the debate here as usual lags that of the northern hemisphere by several years.*

"'At the heart of this is the return of great power conflict to the centre of Western security concerns, and this is something where nuclear weapons simply cannot be ignored as an integral part of the problem, and how we will manage it.*

"'NATO's re-focus on collective defence since 2014 has brought with it a revival of institutional and governmental interest in, and engagement with the practical and political aspects of the Alliance's nuclear posture* *and deterrence, in a way we have last seen during the Cold War 30 years ago.*

"'At its recent Brussels summit, the alliance reiterated that "If the fundamental security of any of its members were to be threatened, NATO has the capabilities and resolve to impose costs on an adversary that would be unacceptable and far outweigh the benefits that any adversary could hope to achieve."

"'As the Alliance re-examines the role of nuclear weapons in a coherent deterrence posture, it re-discovers old realisations such as that nuclear use by NATO should be remote, but should also not be left to the point where it ceases to be a choice; and that if there is not to be an option for conventional victory over NATO, NATO does need a credible nuclear option.

"'In Asia, the return of nuclear weapons is less obvious since there is no nuclear alliance in the way that NATO is. Interest in nuclear deterrence, and possibly a domestic capability, in Japan and South Korea has now been part of the regional security landscape for quite some time....

What does all of this mean for Australia though?

"'First, in a world in which we are concerned primarily about conflict with and between nuclear great powers, and the role of Australian strike in such a situation, we need to think seriously about war termination. When we look at long range and precision strike in a defence force that has some of the shiniest kit available in its inventory, there is always a danger of tactical enthusiasm trumping strategic logic.

"'This isn't a completely new problem, in that strategic guidance during the 1970s and 1980s was always somewhat cautious about the role of strategic strike in a conflict with Indonesia. But that was a question not about what Australia could do in a war with Jakarta, but what would be prudent to do, given that war is ultimately about the nature of the peace that follows.

"'Now, however, we also need to acknowledge the operational limits of a conventional force. At the time of the 2009 White Paper, which mentioned land-attack cruise missiles for our submarines, there was certainly some rather silly debate, I think, which ignored the rather large delta between the damage that a few dozen of half-ton warheads can do to a nation of a billion people, and what might be required to force an end to hostilities on Australia's terms.

"'Some gaps are simply too big to fill with power point slides on Effects Based Operations.

"'When we contemplate conflict with a nuclear armed great power, we face an adversary that will always be able to take greater losses, and inflict more pain, on us than we are able to on them. Conflict will end not because of Australia could force an end to it, but because of the outcome of campaigns elsewhere, or because the cost-benefit calculation of the adversary shifts to make continuing conflict with Australia not worth the bother.

"'This means we need to think about strike in a way that does not reinforce the adversary's emotional investment in the conflict with Australia, while still increasing the cost of any offensive operations they might choose to undertake against us. In that sense, I think the geographic limits of Australian independent strike, given the range of F-111 and current airborne systems, up to the Northern ends, but not much beyond the Indonesian archipelago, still make a lot of sense, even if the adversary's main base areas are located further to the North.

"'But it means that within that geographic envelope, the volume and intensity of strike we can deliver will be particularly important, as the adversary will be able to concentrate at a time and place of their choosing. And when Australia's theory of victory has to rest on exhausting the adversary, attrition will be the name of the game, including attrition of ADF strike assets.

"'Where do nuclear weapons play into this?

"'It is useful to think about the role of nuclear weapons in three differ-ent ways:

- *First, as a complement to conventional forces, bypassing the force-on-force battle to deliver a level of societal damage suffi-cient to induce war termination on their own.*

- *Second, as a tactical substitute for conventional forces, which thanks to their yield-to weight ratios are able to deliver physical damage to major units and installations with an incompara-bly smaller number of ordnances than could ever be achieved with conventional means.*

- *And third, in a strategy of flexible response, though use or threat of limited use, to deter or to bring about an escalation of conflict, so that we can manage the perception of cost and ben-efit for an adversary in the hope of forcing an end of hostilities, with an endstate that manages to avoid the two perils of defeat as well as of a general nuclear war.*

"'It is a complement to conventional forces that nuclear weapons are sometimes referred to as "the deterrent." But to be deterred is a choice by the adversary, there is nothing mechanical about it and we need to be very careful in how we use that term in relation to Australia's strike capability.

"'Deterrence works by making threats of unacceptable counteraction in advance of bad things happening, which is not even necessarily a kind of relationship we would want to have with our neighbours even if we might be able to inflict that level of punishment.

"'Therefore, the formulation in some earlier strategic guidance doc-uments of the ADF needing to be of a size and capability to always

command respect and induce caution in adversaries is a more modest, but politically more appropriate, and strategically more credible way of thinking about ADF strike, unless and until we swap the explosive end of our ordnance for something a bit more powerful.

"'Thinking about nuclear weapons as a substitute for conventional forces on the other hand brings us to that stress-test of a purely conventional ADF that I mentioned earlier. Given what we know already about Chinese interest in developing potential base facilities abroad, and as we are talking about the long timespans relevant to the acquisition of major capability, we need to assume that the adversary will already have established air or naval bases in Australia's approaches at the outset of a conflict.

"'Given the size of Chinese armed forces and the nature of its installation already existing in Djibouti, we need to assume that these will be garrisoned to a size that will preclude amphibious operations as a means to destroy such bases. Hence, we're back to a replay of the Rabaul campaign under modern conditions, which will require sustained strike against an adversary that will be prepared, hardened, dispersed, and able to inflict attrition on Australian forces.

"'Even before we take into account the need to also meet adversary manoeuvre forces, I think it is very doubtful whether we could ever acquire cruise missile stocks large enough for such a campaign. While we might in future buy enough fighter-bombers to afford attrition over time, the question is how many tankers we could afford to lose before such a campaign unravels. If we think about stress-testing our current force mix in that way, I think we thus need to come to three conclusions:

"'First, we will in coming decades have a need for a survivable long-range bomb truck, of a kind where the new U.S. long-range bomber is probably the only airframe currently on the horizon that approximates our requirements.

"'Second, when push comes to shove, there may well be targets in Southeast Asia where the unrivalled yield-weight advantages of nuclear weapons would provide significant military benefit to an allied campaign.

"'Third, the archipelago of Southeast Asia is the one area in the broader Indo-Pacific area where the most opportune targets for initial allied nuclear strikes will be located if the United States looks to escalate a conflict to the nuclear level.

"'This third point may seem like a bit of a leap, but a logical conclusion if one eliminates the alternatives. Like their Soviet predecessors, Chinese bases in the Indian Ocean are so exposed to U.S. forces from the Atlantic that they are unlikely to remain in play for very long. If we and the Americans roll-up Chinese forces in Southeast Asia, the war doesn't seem to be going so badly that the U.S. and its allies would look to nuclear use. And Northeast Asia is so proximate to major population centres of both sides, and unlikely to feature adversary bases outside the Chinese homeland itself, so that any nuclear use up there would make for far more challenging escalation control.

"'Given that Australia has most to lose from enduring adversary presence in our approaches—Japan's control of the German mandate islands after World War One comes to mind as something worth remembering—we might not actually be that unhappy about such a development.

"'Hence, if we are looking at the effectiveness and role of strike in general in our region, there are reasons why I think it behoves on us to study the tactical as well as strategic and political considerations of nuclear use in our approaches in much greater detail than we have done since the 1950s.

"'The first is that we probably understand the limits of conventional forces in a contemporary maritime context far better than the potential

advantages of nuclear use, whether that is Australian or more likely U.S. use. The earliest influence of nuclear weapons on the conduct of naval operations was during the Korean War, when the U.S. fleet at Pusan was spaced so as to minimise the damage from airborne Soviet nuclear attack. For reasons of effectiveness, low collateral damage and relative ease of escalation control, tactical nuclear weapons remained fundamental to naval concepts of operation in the Atlantic until the end of the Cold War.

"'But while it is easy to see how nuclear weapons remain effective against fixed installations, are they as effective in a naval context today as they were then, given the extent to which modern air and naval forces can disperse in a networked environment anyway?

"'Without understanding the tactical benefit of nuclear weapons, we cannot have an informed discussion of the relevance to the defence of Australia or the defence of Southeast Asia, or what a 'militarily meaningful' initial use of nuclear weapons by the United States might look like, which Australia would have to look to if conventional strike capabilities are exhausted.

"'And if the history of the debates between Australian, U.S. and UK planners in SEATO days is any guide, our assessment of their benefit in our particular circumstances does not necessarily align with that of our allies.

"'Second, well short of those considerations of actual use, we do have to ask how Australian independent strike capabilities relate to the need for demonstrating a credible US capacity for nuclear escalation and intra-war deterrence in our region. Nuclear signalling, coercion, and the dispersion of nuclear forces to maintain credible options for limited use have been part of major crises between peer great powers throughout the atomic age and will remain so in the future.

"'In any major crisis with China, the United States will look to Australia as a dispersal area for long-range air assets, and that will bring with it nuclear connotations whether we like it or not.

"'If our strategic circumstances continue to deteriorate, we may well welcome this and even seek greater physical linkage with U.S. nuclear forces in the way that exist in NATO, and Japan and South Korea have explored for some time. But Australian strike forces will be of relevance to nuclear signalling well short of nuclear sharing.

"'In contemplating Australian independent strike in a conflict with a nuclear power, we will be operating aircraft or weapons systems that might be very difficult if not impossible for the other side to distinguish from US nuclear capable systems, and the question of whether and how Australian forces might be called upon to support US nuclear operations from and in our region, if only for signalling, will pose difficult political questions that we have not had to deal with in our alliance yet.

"'In conclusion, nuclear warfare and strategy are about the ability to deliver massed violence, but exactly for that reason they always also induce a measure and need for restraint. In those scenarios that will seriously test our force, and our defence posture and policy overall—in other words, those scenarios where independent strike really counts—we will not be able to escape the shadow of nuclear deterrence.

"'Hence, when thinking about the future of Australian strike in the shadow of nuclear weapons, we will need to be able to deliver a far greater volume of massed violence at range than we are able to at present—we will also have to think a lot harder about when and where it would be

more prudent to exercise restraint when we come to heads with nuclear powers. ”[23]

---

23. https://defence.info/re-thinking-strategy/2018/09/deterrence-in-the-australian-evolving-strategic-environment-the-perspective-of-dr-stephan-Frühling/

Chapter Ten

Conclusion

Perhaps using the term conclusion is a misnomer. The subject of reshaping Australian defence is in the period of relaunch and in a period of significant historical change. Although an island continent which is located at the end of the Pacific, it is now deeply enmeshed in the global change affecting the reshaping of the global system.

It has become a central player in how the Chinese way of reshaping global power plays out, whether it wants to be or not. It is significant enough to set its own course but not powerful enough to do so unilaterally.

And it needs a defence policy that fits this period of global upheaval. In my view, it is by becoming more resilient and doing so by being interactive with and driving change amongst its allies to shape credible paths to more resilience in the face of the authoritarian powers that it provides a leadership role.

I discussed this shift with Ross Babbage most recently in my April 2023 visit. Here, he highlighted what he considers to be three key elements in Australia to being able to shape a broader defence capability. For Babbage, shaping a broader defence capability is not just about the ADF and its own operational capability. "If you're looking at it from Beijing's point of view, they'd have to think very carefully about messing with us for we do have a very capable although small military and we have even more powerful friends." But the ADF lacks strategic depth and sustainability. As Babbage noted: "We are in danger of being a one-month operational military in case of conflict due to the lack of economic and industrial depth, such as the provision of fuels and key munitions and spare parts."

The second aspect for Australia is its alliance structure. As Babbage underscored, Australia has focused upon ramping up its alliance working relationships to the point where its own forces can more effectively integrate with the Americans and are working towards greater cooperation with other allies as well, notably the Japanese. The result is clear: "The sum of alliance efforts is greater than any of the parts. This is a consideration which Beijing has to realize is not working to its advantage. The Chinese threat has drawn many nations in the Pacific closer together to resist authoritarian interference." And it is not just about Pacific allies: a number of European states have woken up to the realisation that China directly threatens their interests, and they have to find ways to contribute to the deterrence of China as well. Babbage noted: "We will cooperate with a range of others, including a number of relatively powerful and capable Europeans with whom we have long-standing partnerships."

And that led to the discussion of the third element in Australian deterrence, developing more effective regional partnerships. Here he discussed evolving relationships with India, Indonesia, and other Southeast Asian and South Pacific countries. Australia is working hard to develop closer military, security, economic, technological, and diplomatic relationships that can strengthen regional cooperation and deterrence. Working with its neighbourhood much more directly and effectively is a key part of shaping the way ahead for Australia's deterrence strategy.

The challenge is to move from the near and midterm efforts at enhanced national military capability and allied interoperability to a stronger capability for resilient societies that empower enduring forces, not just one-month militaries. The close allies need to review and restructure their strategic supply chains as a matter of urgency to reinforce each other's economic and industrial strengths and cover their respective weaknesses.

New levels of allied cooperation are required along with new planning and management mechanisms. These initiatives are needed urgently if the allies are to have a credible deterrent going forward and if they are going to be able to endure and sustain themselves in the event of a major conflict.

Australia's ability to enhance its ability for the direct defence of the continent while working with allies to operate as a sanctuary in times of crisis is the key way ahead. My colleague Dr. Andrew Carr has highlighted a way to think about this path to the future.

"In recent years much has been made of Australia's decision to acquire long-range nuclear-powered submarines, its desire for 'interchangeable' forces with America and the claim by a former Defence Minister that it would be 'inconceivable' Australia would not be involved in a conflict over Taiwan.

"However, any expectation that Australia is on the verge of joining a grand military coalition to counter-balance China in Northeast Asia should be dashed after a close reading of Australia's new 2023 National Defence: Defence Strategic Review.. Sobered by the realities of China's rapid military growth and conscious that Washington is 'no longer the unipolar leader of the Indo-Pacific' as well as the limits of political and military support in the region for confrontational strategies, a new form of allied cooperation is emerging.

"For Australia, this is the era of Archipelagic Deterrence. Canberra is building a secure southern bastion in order to deter and deny China's military any coercive role within the archipelagic zone from the north-eastern Indian Ocean, through maritime Southeast Asia and into the South Pacific. At the same time, Canberra is relinquishing decades of guarded sovereignty, and allowing the United States to significantly expand its military footprint in Australia so as to better project power into Asia. Beginning with a U.S. Marine presence in 2011, Australia is now allowing 'the rotational deployment of U.S. aircraft of all types in Australia,' establishing facilities to regularly host U.S. nuclear-powered submarines and building 'a combined logistics, sustainment and maintenance enterprise to support high-end warfighting and combined military operations in the region.'

"To achieve the strategy of Archipelagic Deterrence, three big challenges Australia will have to overcome. First is the construction of deterrence systems. Along with the political-strategic effort to establish credibility and communication, significant new military capabilities are being acquired, including an Anti-Access/Area Denial (A2/AD) shield, and the AUKUS nuclear powered submarines.

"Second, Australia's strategic geography must evolve. In place of viewing Australia as a clearly delineated island nation with a defensive 'moat,' a flexible archipelagic sense of place is emerging. Australia's defence forces now seek to move seamlessly and rapidly across the littorals of Australia's northern shores and into the region, utilising a series of island-like 'nodes' and a dispersed network of bases and logistics facilities.

"Third and finally, to align strategy and geography to force structure, Australian defence planning has embraced net assessment. This

U.S. Cold War era strategic tool is being repurposed in an unusual way in order to break away from a problematic capability acquisition processes and create a 'focused force' for specific scenarios.

"Australia's Archipelagic Deterrence strategy represents a more stable and resilient alignment of interests and capabilities between Canberra and Washington than forward-leaning alternatives. Australian leaders may talk loudly about pan-regional and global contributions; however, the enduring logic of the nation's force structure and posture has always been territorial security. The 2023 DSR reinforces that tradition, with the Australian government insisting on the need to 'sharpen our focus, on what our interests are, and how to uphold them' in the face of the gravitational pull of attention towards the U.S.-China competition.

"Recognition of this enduring thread of distinct Australian strategic interests will frustrate those hoping rich allies will help Washington to directly lift the military burden from its tired and distracted shoulders. So too for those who believe only allied boots on the ground in Taiwan can prevent its takeover.

"However, Archipelagic Deterrence, with its creation of a secure southern bastion around Australia, deeply integrated with U.S. power projection into the region is likely to be better suited to the realities of distinct interests and capacities and ultimately will be more valuable to the management of major power strategic competition in the Indo-Pacific."

In short, shaping a way ahead for Australian defence in an increasingly contested Indo-Pacific region revolves around Australia's in anchoring the capabilities of the liberal democracies to survive and thrive against the twenty-first-century authoritarians, with China as a key driver of change.

Chapter Eleven

Additional Books

Joint by Design: The Evolution of Australian Defence Strategy

This book although focused on Australia, is not just about Australia. The strategic shift from the land wars to full spectrum crisis management requires the liberal democracies to have forces lethal enough, survivable enough, and agile enough to support full spectrum crisis management.

What is being shaped is an integrated distributed force able to operate through interactive kill webs. Because the Australian Defence Force is small but operating in many ways the most modern Air Force in the democratic world, they have focused on force integration as a key necessity to achieve the desired combat effect.

Because Australia's allies now realise that they too need to follow this path, the Aussies have been at the cutting edge of thinking about the changes the military forces of the liberal democracies must make.

This is why this book although about Australia, is really about shaping a way ahead for the liberal democratic military forces. This book has come to fruition through Laird's involvement in the Williams Foundation, and the work he has done with the foundation since 2014.

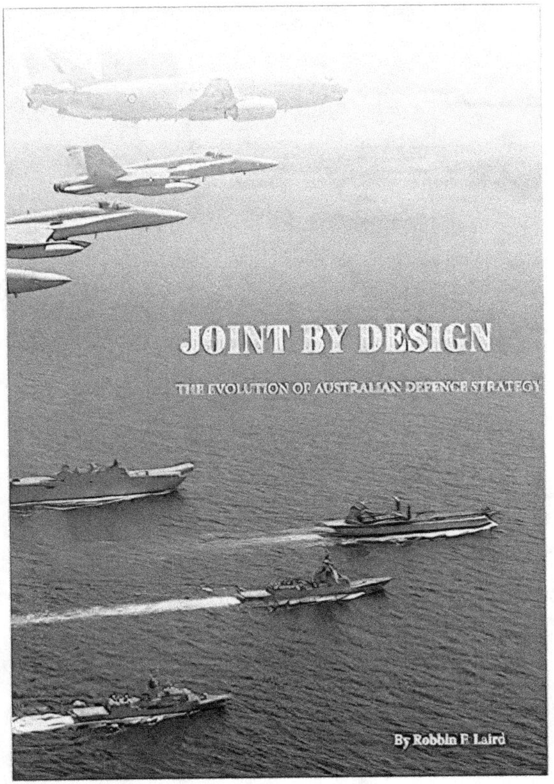

The foundation has held two public seminars—focusing on the rebuilding of the Australian Defence Force and the intersection between this rebuilding process and the evolution of the strategic environment—each year since 2015, and he wrote the reports for these seminars.

The book focuses on how Australia has updated its defence and security strategy since 2014, as seen through the lens of these Williams Foundation seminars. The book begins with an introduction to the path of change, and then addresses the context and the nature of the changes put in place each year. The book concludes with a discussion on how the Australian strategy as reshaped by the Morrison Administration generated a broader response to the challenges posed by the Chinese in the Indo-Pacific region.

The book focuses on the period from 2014 through 2020 when Australia shut down to deal with the pandemic.

As one reviewer commented about the book: "It is obvious that Laird is not a simple military and security analyst. By reading his book, it turns out that thanks to his editorial work, he is also an experienced narrator with the necessary skillset to tell a complex story in an exciting way. Therefore, overall, it is important to note that *Joint by Design: The Evolution of the Australian Defence Strategy* is not just an academic book that develops the context and the making of the new defence and security strategy of Australia, but because of the wealth of reports about seminars and quotes from key actors, it is also a very credible source for historians. This is particularly valuable when its main topic is one into which it is very rare to gain such deep and detailed insight."

Defense XXII: A World in Transition

Published in May 2023, this is the third annual publication we have published at *Second Line of Defense* and *Defense Information*.

Each publication highlights themes from essays we have published during that year. We are living in a time of compressed history, and our essays try to capture the history emerging in that year. We focus on defense issues, so we have highlighted some of the key developments affecting the evolution of defense and security challenges facing the United States and its key allies in that year, as well as innovations and developments in selected military technologies and concepts of operations.

The first volume was titled *2020: A Pivotal Year? Navigating Strategic Change at a Time of COVID-19 Disruption*. The book focused on the impact of COVID-19 and the strategic change evidenced in 2020. The 2020 book focused on the pandemic, notably as it played out in France and Britain. The book provided an overview of the challenge of navigating strategic change at a time of COVID-19 disruption.

The second volume was titled *Defense XXI: Shaping a Way Ahead for the United States and its Key Allies*. The book focused on the key drivers of change in defense, which are reshaping force capabilities, and the strategic context within which those capabilities are being shaped. It is about technology, concepts of operations, and strategic purposes for defense.

One theme we explored in 2021 was the increased challenge to the liberal democratic order from authoritarian powers. This is a major theme in this volume. We have focused on how major allies are changing their focus on how to defend themselves in the context of their broader alliances.

As the noted military novelist and author, George Galdorisi has noted:

"*Defense XXII: A World in Transition* is one of those rare books focused on political, diplomatic and military matters that will appeal to experts in the field as well as the layperson. Robbin Laird has assembled a breathtaking array of professionals and has woven together a narrative that makes this book unique. It reads like a novel, and you just have to turn to the next page to see what happens next.

"To say that this book is topical is an understatement. Unsurprisingly, initial lessons learned from the conflict in Ukraine loom large.

That said, rather than just repeating what has been reported on this conflict in the media, *Defense XXII* takes a well-nuanced deep-dive into the war's lessons learned, and then goes a step further by assessing how this war will impact global security in the years ahead.

"Importantly, this book unpacks Russian leader, Vladimir Putin's, motivations, goals, and objectives for launching Europe's most destructive war three-quarters of a century. While no one can read Putin's mind, the analysis provided in *Defense XXII* goes a long way in sorting the wheat from the chaff in understanding not only why what occurred in Ukraine happened, but what is likely to transpire next.

"What makes *Defense XXII* especially appealing is the way that the editor is able to seamlessly weave together dozens of interviews, statements, speeches and his own opinions in a way that gives the reader an opportunity to make up his or her mind on an array of issues that not only stem from today's headlines, but ones that will impact nations for years, if not decades.

"Few books are both readable and informative, but *Defense XXII: A World in Transition* is that rare book that hits that mark."

Books of Dr. Laird

Scientific-Technological Revolution and Soviet Foreign Policy. (Co-author Erik Hoffmann). 1982.

The Soviet Union and Strategic Arms. 1984 (Co-author Dale Herspring).

The Soviet Polity in the Modern Era (Co-edited with Erik Hoffmann). 1984.

Technocratic Socialism: The Soviet Union in the Advanced Industrial Era (Co-author Erik Hoffmann). 1985.

French Security Policy in Transition: Dynamics of Continuity and Change. 1985.

France, The Soviet Union, And the Nuclear Weapons Issue. 1985. Reissued by Routledge, 2020.

Perspectives on Defense futures : National Developments in Europe. (Jim Lacy co-author). 1985.

French Security Policy: From Independence to Interdependence. 1986. Reissued by Routledge in 2020.

The Soviet Union, the West, and the Nuclear Arms Race. 1986.

Soviet Foreign Policy. (Editor). 1987

Strangers & Friends, the Franco German Security Relationship. 1989

The Future of Deterrence: NATO Nuclear Forces After INF. 1990 (Co-editor Betsy Jacobs). Reissued by Routledge in 2021.

USSR and the Western Alliance (Susan Clark co-editor). 1990. Reissued by Routledge in 2022.

The Europeanization of The Alliance. 1991. Reissued by Routledge in 2021.

Soviet Foreign Policy: Classic and Contemporary Issues. 1991 (Co-editors Erik Hoffmann and Fred Fleron).

The Soviets, Germany, And the New Europe. 1992. Reissued by Routledge in 2021.

The Revolution in Military Affairs: Allied Perspectives (Co-author Holger Mey). 2004

Contemporary Issues in Soviet Foreign Policy: From Brezhnev to Gorbachev. 2008 Reissued by Routledge. (Co-editors Erik Hoffmann and Fred Fleron).

Three Dimensional Warriors: Second Edition. 2013

Rebuilding American Military Power in the Pacific: A 21st-Century Strategy. 2013. (Co-authors Ed Timperlake and Richard Weitz).

The F-35 and 21st Century Defence. 2016

Training for the High-End Fight: The Strategic Shift of the 2020s. 2021.

2020: A Pivotal Year?: Navigating Strategic Change at a Time of Covid-19 Disruption (Editor). 2021.

Joint by Design: The Evolution of Australian Defence Strategy. 2021

The Return of Direct Defense in Europe: Meeting the 21st Century Authoritarian Challenge. (Co-author Murielle Delaporte). 2020.

The U.S. Marine Corps Transformation Path: Preparing for the High-End Fight. 2022.

A Maritime Kill Web Force in the Making: Deterrence and Warfighting in the 21st Century (Co-author Ed Timperlake). 2022

Defense XXI: Shaping a Way Ahead for the United States and Its Allies. (Editor) 2022.

Defense XXII: A World in Transition (Editor). 2023.

The Role of the Osprey in the Pivot to the Pacific. 2023.

Kenneth Maxwell on Global Trends: An Historian of the 18th Century Looks at the Contemporary World (Editor). 2023

Australian Defence and Deterrence: A 2023 Update. 2023

The Coming of the CH-53K : A New Capability for the Distributed Force. 2023.

Articles Published Between 2002 and 2013 on Strategic Issues

Capabilities Based Procurement (2002)

Industry Transformation (2002)

Transformation and the Defense Industrial Base: A New Model (2003)

Big Questions Hover Over U.S. Space Industry (2003)

Rules to Navigate the Way Ahead in Military Space (2004)

Redesigning The Space Industrial Base: Reflections on The Aldridge Commission (2004) EU-US Co-Opetition: 10

Trends for the Future (2005)

Logistics Is an Emerging Strategic Issue for Military Planners (2005)

Maritime Security: New Requirements for Global Collaboration (2005)

The NRO and the USAF: Integration in Search of a Purpose (2005)

Transformed Logistics: An Interview with Mike Wynne (2005)

The Challenge to Congress and NASA: Building a Successful Space Program Together (2006)

Fixing Space Acquisition: From Spiral Development To Cookie-Cutter Production (2006)

Beyond "Back to Basics" (2007)

Framing a Mission Architecture: An Interview with USCG Admiral John Currier (2007)

Shaping Hands-On Coalition Capability at Sea (2007) Testing the Concepts, Refining the Approaches: LOGMOD-2007-2 (2007)

New Possibilities in Space for U.S., France (2007)

Crafting 21 st Century Air Battle Management: A Critical Deterrent in the Middle East (2008)

Evolving Defence Business Models: Challenges of Globalisation, Systems Integration and National Interests (2008)

The Future of Military Space (2008)

Global C4ISR Evolves (2008)

The USMC and the Sea Base Enterprise (2008)

The Future of Military Space (2008)

The Maritime Trade Dynamic: Reshaping the US Coast Guard Role (2008)

The Connectivity Opportunity (2009)

A 21st -century Concept of Air and Military Operations (2009)

The Nation Ignores the Defense Industry In Its Quest For An 'Economic Stimulus' (2009)

Shaping future strategic capability: the f-35 Manufacturing Approach (2009)

The Strategic Impact of the Financial Crisis on Space (2009)

Leveraging Austerity: Re-crafting Military Space (2009) The Case for New Programmes in a Period of Defence Transition: The Naval Unmanned Combat Air System Case (2009)

Shaping the Sustainment Enterprise (2010)

U.S. Strategy 2020: Facing a Multipolar Future (2010)

Osprey Maintenance Moves Forward (2010) Three Dimensional Warriors (Abbreviated Version) (2011)

Reshape U.S. Force Structure for Agility (2011)

Embrace the Air-Power Revolution (2011)

Building Blocks for a New U.S. Military Space Policy (2011)

Leveraging New Platforms During the Strategic Transition (2011)

Meeting the Challenge of Maritime Security (2011)

Search and Rescue: Why the Coast Guard Needs Help (2011)

Shaping Arctic Strategy (2012)

Bold Alligator 2012: Re-Shaping Maneuver Warfare from the Sea (2012)

The Space Impact of the Euro Crisis (2012)

V-22 Osprey: Expanding the Operational Space (2012)

Shaping Redundant Response U.S. Military Space Capabilities (2012)

Shaping the Battlespace: Osprey, F-35B Vital to Sea Base Operations (2012)

Shaping Marine Corps Aviation's Future in the MAGTF: The VMX-22 Contribution (2013)

Pivot Point: Re-shaping U.S. Maritime Strategy to the Pacific (2013)[1]

---

1. These articles can be read here:
https://defense.info/highlight-of-the-week/looking-back-articles-and-studies-published-between-2002-and-2013/